What My Students Taught Me

Letters from My Time in Teaching

DAVID J FISHKIND

Fulton Books, Inc.
Meadville, PA

Published by Fulton Books 2021

ISBN 978-1-63860-287-3 (paperback)
ISBN 978-1-63860-288-0 (digital)

Printed in the United States of America

This book is dedicated to my soul mate, Roxy, without whom the book would have no title. Her positive influence on me cannot be encompassed in this small space. This book is also dedicated to *all* my students who have *ever* been in my classroom. Whether they are in the book or not, they have a place and have made an impact on me!

Author's Note

Greetings! Thank you for choosing my book. I appreciate it very much. This book is about what teaching can do. It was said long ago by a very wise person that "to teach is to touch a life forever." Truer words were never spoken. The pages of this book contain actual letters I have received over the latter part of my teaching career. They will show a full range of emotions and demonstrate how true the quote really is.

Prologue

I had heard the quote many years before I ever set foot in a class-room—"To teach is to touch a life forever." I had had already had a more-than-twenty-year career in the corporate world. The bulk of that career was spent with an organization that holds a very special place in my heart. The experiences I had there and the people I worked with, both in and outside of that company, helped shape and prepare me for the career I was trained for at Boston State Teacher's College. I graduated in 1980 into an economy that was way down; and the only teaching job available for a new teacher was in Oklahoma, on a Native American reservation.

And as much as I was eager to begin my career, I was not pre-pared to uproot myself and start for so little money. I was not ready, which is why the corporate career was taken first. I had to "get it out of my system," and the joke I always told myself is that I would work for a lumber company (Somerville Lumber) until "something better came along." Well, it took seventeen years, and the company being killed by Home Depot for me to begin gravitating toward teach-ing. And so, after three years in software (went through an IPO in a start-up), a year in telecom, and two years in import-export, it was time.

And this is how it began. It began on a Monday morning after I had been on vacation. I was listening to the morning sales meeting; and in the middle, I closed my laptop, shoved it across the table, and said, "I quit." The open mouths and vacant expressions told me it was the right time. I got to my home at that time, and my then-fian-cée asked me what the hell I was doing home. I said that I had quit my job as I was sick of the politics.

Then, I took our Belgian Malinois for a walk; and as I went up the street, I met our neighbor, Harry, who was a guidance counselor at a high school in Homestead. It was the first week of August. He said, "What are you doing home?" I told him I had just quit my corporate job, and he said, "Why don't you come down to the school and apply for a teaching job?"

And so I did.

And the rest, as they say, is history. Miami-Dade County Public Schools was a bit of a bumpy ride as there was little in the way of direction. The school was great (it had the distinction of being the only building left standing after Hurricane Andrew) but had a challenging population. The poverty there was readily evident, but the students showed that the desire to learn does not know economics. And that is the opening that was needed. I gave them skills, had them practice and employ them, and they saw results.

After seven years in Dade, I moved to Broward County, which is a completely different world. From the moment I began, the whole atmosphere was so much more positive. I began at a for-profit Charter 6-12 educational center in Lauderhill. It was an eye-opening view of what charter schools are about. I saw so much in the time I was there from the second half of a school year (I began in January) to April (when the school told us they were missing payroll) to the second time they did this (end of April) when two-thirds of the faculty quit in protest. This left me and one other English teacher to handle the *entire* enrollment of sixth-grade to twelfth-grade students. At one point in early May, I was teaching simultaneously English 1, 2, 3, and 4 and Honors *and* AP, and this was done in the school cafeteria.

I literally had to run from table to table, giving assignments, checking on them, and collecting (and grading) *all* that work, along with quizzes, tests, and final exams.

The year ended, and the school asked me to assume the duties of department head. I spent that summer trying to get into the public schools, and despite numerous interviews, I ended the summer with no new job and returned to the ill-fated charter school. I say ill-fated for this reason: on the first day of school, enrollment was noticeably down, and we had a faculty meeting after the first day. As the meeting started, our principal, who was a very well-dressed and well-spoken woman who possessed two doctorates, proceeded to interrupt the chairman of the board, cursed him out in a way that would make a truck driver blush, and quit. There were a lot of open mouths around the meeting floor. Just after Labor Day, we had an "emergency" faculty meeting called, and the chairman informed us that due to falling enrollment that the school would be closing on Friday (two days after this meeting).

I told my wife this when I got home, and while we were running an errand, she asked, "What are you going to do?"

Whereupon the phone rang before I could answer. It was Mr. Most, one of the APs from Everglades High School. He said, "I know it's short notice, but can you come in for an interview tomorrow at 4:30?"

I said absolutely.

The universe has a way of opening a door when one is closing. I went to the interview, which consisted of Mr. Most and Dr. Cash, the department chair for language arts. Typically, these interviews last about fifteen to twenty minutes. Mine was over an hour based on one question. They asked me if I knew how to differentiate instruction.

I chuckled and told them about teaching four sections of English simultaneously in the cafeteria. The open mouths told me I had a really good chance of getting the job. It ended with him telling me he would let me know tomorrow.

So I woke up on that fateful Friday, drove to the charter school, and was confronted with three news trucks, covering the closing of the school. The last thing an educator wants to see is a news truck in the driveway of their school, let alone three. I entered to children crying (some had been there since sixth grade), parents yelling, and administrators running away from them. I gathered all my students into a large classroom and told them just to keep doing the things that made them successful and that they would all be okay in their "home" schools. At nine forty-five that morning my phone rang, and it was Mr. Most again. "Okay, you've got the job. Get yourself downtown as soon as possible!" It was a scene right out of *Apocalypse Now* as I told my administrator, who said, "Take me with you!" laughed, and wished me luck.

I landed at Everglades High School and began the best days of my teaching career. Over the course of the nine school years I was at Everglades, I was fortunate enough to teach the following courses: English 1, English 1 honors, English 2, English 2 honors, English 3, creative writing (I wrote the curriculum for the course and taught it for two years before handing it off), intensive reading, and finally credit recover. It is arguable that I worked with the most diverse groups the school had to offer. The pages inside will tell you the rest. Know that only the great pandemic of 2020 forced my retirement a year and a half early.

This book is about the letters, which were given to me over the years, along with an assignment where I had the students rate my performance over the course of the school year in which they had me as their instructor. I took two things from the many, many continuing education courses (forty-seven courses) I took over the years.

One came from Harry Wong, who encouraged teachers to "get to know their students early," which I accomplished via a first-day assignment called "getting to know you" where I had the students write ten to fifteen sentences about themselves. In that short written space, I observed language and structure diagnostics, a glimpse into their character and life, and ways to build bridges essential to get them to "buy in" on education. The second assignment, done at the end of the year, allowed for the students to rate my performance, without restrictions (okay, they could not use curse words), and I told them to be honest! There were always some interesting responses, which I will share with you. The student names will not be revealed; but the year and section will be, along with initials. So sit back, read and enjoy the journey!

Everglades High School (School Year 2014–2015)
Courses Taught: English 2 Regular and Creative Writing
End-of-Year Ratings from English 2 Students by Period

===

Period 1
End of Year Rating and Notes

May 27, 2015
Professionalism—10, Preparedness—10, Personality—10

Mr. Fishkind, you are very professional in terms of your career, and it is very obvious that professionalism was acquired through experience. You are always prepared, and I appreciate the fact that you always have a plan B. If I were to give you anything less than a 10 in terms of personality, it would be crazy because you're spewing it.

—AD

///

May 27, 2015
Ratings 9.5 across the board

Mr. Fishkind, the rating of your overall performance in terms of preparedness, professionalism, and personality, you did very well and performed in a mature & in a calm & collected manner. In terms of preparedness, you got your things in shape & you always have your stuff where it needs to be. In terms of professionalism, you were very professional in what you are doing in your career as an English II teacher. You have a gratuitous amount of vocabulary & you enforce rules a=in a calm & lively manner. In terms of personality, you have a unique and wonderful personality, & you are great with a guitar!

You have an acquired taste in music & you are an outstanding poet!

You are the most professional & the most mature out of the other teachers I have. You are my favorite. I rate you a 9.5/10. Keep up the good work you do every day to change people's lives…

—GA

===

May 28, 2015

This year you were prepared every day, even in case of set-back events. You always had everything written on the board and were ready to explain. You are also very professional because if you do have personal issues at home, you do not let them get in the way of your teaching. You also handle situations very calmly. Personality-wise, you are one of the best teachers I have ever had…

—JA

//

May 27, 2015

Mr. Fishkind, your performance was perfect. There was nothing wrong with anything, only the amount of work you gave us, but other than that, just perfect…

—AC

===

May 27, 2015

Mr. Fishkind, you are the most prepared teacher I have ever had. You always expect the unexpected and prepare for any situation. You also have a chill personality, that when the time is needed, can turn strict, which helps a lot when comes to doing work and getting help.

—DE

//

May 27, 2015
Rate 9 of 10

Reason: I would have given you a 10 out of 10, but I'm not a big fan of English. I have always had a bad history with English teachers. I don't know but you just made me enjoy a little more and you as a teacher, are great. You also help me a lot this year and I really appreciate that. I don't say this very often to teachers, but I hope you have a great life and I'll miss having you as a teacher. THANK YOU!! ☺

—ID

==

May 27, 2015

IN my point of view, the teacher is an excellent professional, who knows how to teach and understand their class topic that is being discussed. His personality makes him look like a student, but as it takes time to teach and laugh with us, but never leave his role as a teacher. To finalize, the preparation that gives us excellent vocabulary with their classes and learn much more…

—HG

//

May 27, 2015
Rating—8

If I were to rate your performance from a rate of 1–10, I would rate it an 8. First, because of his patience & the time he takes to teach us. Also, because of his quality of instruction. I understand what he is saying.

—DG

===

May 27, 2015

Mr. Fishkind, as far as preparation, you prepared us fairly well for the EOC testing. I wish we could have gone over some more techniques. As for professionalism, you were very professional this year, and yet we were still able to laugh and joke around, which goes to show your personality, which is wonderful!

—JG

//

May 27, 2015
Preparedness—10, Professionalism—10, Personality—10+

Preparedness—Mr. Fishkind always prepare us beforehand, which helps us out in the long run.
Professionalism—Even though he's cool, he's still professional and we respect him.
Personality—His personality is what makes him one of my favorite teachers in my 2014–2015 school year.

—IJB

===

May 27, 2015

Preparedness: 10—Always ready to work, always on time, and always knows what he's going to be doing for every class.
Professionalism: 9 ½—I give that rating because when kids make you mad/upset, you get out of character (ex. cursing).
Note: In all my time on a classroom, I never swore in front of students, except in Russian.

Personality—10 only because you're a morning person, and you woke me up in the morning with music and different voices.

—DM

///

May 27, 2015

Hello, Mr. Fishkind, in this warm-up, I will rate your performance in terms of preparedness, professionalism and personality. I can see that you are always prepared for our class ever since the school year started. Your professionalism is good at most times, because I know some of your student's behavior cause you to be unprofessional. Last thing is about you is our personality, but I feel you can easily be stressed or grumpy.

—RM

===

May 27, 2015

Based on professionalism, preparedness and personality, I think you portray them all pretty well! I consider you to always be prepared and have something new to do. As well as professional when it comes to following the rules. I also think you have a lot of personality. In all, I've had a great year with you.

—MP

///

May 27, 2015
Rating—9

I think that throughout the year, you have been an amazing teacher and role model: supportive, smart, understanding and humble. There's not a lot of bad things I could say about one of my favorite teachers. But if I have to, I would say less warm-ups and more time for reading and ticket-outs. And also, when you're in a bad mood with some other students, don't yell! It annoys me, not to be rude, but it is seriously annoying, but keep it up, you're a good teacher!

—PQ

===

May 27, 2015

To rate Mr. Fishkind's performance in terms of preparedness, professionalism and personality, I will be completely honest. In terms of preparedness, he is very shitty in preparing assignments. In terms of professionalism, he's good at what he does. And last, in terms of personality, he can be humorous or very serious, depending upon the situation. So, in preparedness, it would be 2.5 out of 5, in professionalism 5 out of 5 and so is personality.

—RR

//

May 27, 2015

Mr. /Fishkind takes his job very seriously. If I had to rate Mr. Fishkind's performance throughout my school year as extremely professional.

—JR

===

May 27, 2015

Preparedness—prepared everyday
Professionalism—very professional, never angry or cursing
Personality—always joyful

—RR

///

May 27, 2015

To be honest, you are an awesome teacher Mr. Fishkind, because you are always on time, which is an important thing. You're funny, and you like to teach people that want to learn from you. One of the main things about you is we actually work in your class!

—DS

===

May 27, 2015
Preparedness—4.5/5, Professionalism—5/5, Personality—5/5

You never have bene unprepared. You always have your stuff together. Your professional and always organize. You're a very cool teacher and a nice one too!

—AT

///

May 27, 2015
Period 2

10/10—preparedness10/10—professionalism9/10—personality
—JA approved

===

May 27, 2015

Your always prepared and on time. You have an amazing personality. One thing about you everyone loves is that you are honest and straight forward. One thing I struggled to learn about you is that you get mad easily and some days it's easy to get under your skin.

Also, your very neat and responsible. I noticed that you still had the papers from the beginning of the year about our goals.

—CD

//

May 27, 2015

Your performance throughout the school year has been good. In terms of being prepared, Mr. Fishkind always has something for us to do. Mr. Fishkind is always professional and responsible. Mr. Fishkind's personality is good, but some days, it's not the best…

—FG

===

May 27, 2015

I rate your performance this entire year a B+ or B-, due to the fact that you were very much prepared and you was very professional due to the crazy word choice, but your personality honestly killed all the students that attended your class, some referred to you as 'stuck in the 60's.

—KJ

//

May 27, 2015

I would rate Mr. Fishkind as one of the best teachers that I've ever had, because he is always prepared. He knows what to do, and he is always concerned about his students, and if you have some problem, even with homework or something, I'm sure he will be willing to help you. In a scale from 1–10, he is a 10.

—JK

===

May 27, 2015

I find your performance as a teacher excellent, and a fantastic example of how a role model and leader should perform. Your professionalism when I come to the topic of giving aggravated students, students off-task, and the way you do your job is incredible and an amazing feat as all of my other teachers cannot be as professional as you are when it comes to talking to students off task. I find I have grown fond of your wonderful personality as a human being on earth, and as a teacher/friend, and compliments well with your work ethic and style of teacher. I find that your preparedness in teaching is remarkable and stunning as well. If I had to rate you out of 10, I would rate you 100 out of 10, for your manners, personality, preparedness and professionalism.

—JK

//

May 27, 2015

In terms of preparedness, you're spot on. You're ready for everything and anything that might happen, and you have things set up in a way, so everything goes according to plan. In professionalism, you follow all the rules the administrators give you, and you never fail to act accordingly like a teacher. Personality-wise, you're perfect! It's what makes you my favorite teacher, and it's what makes you so appreciated by me (I think I made sense). You've had a great performance all year long, and I'm honestly going to miss that next year.

—LM

===

May 27, 2015

I think this year you were very prepared, because you keep everything in order, and you explained all the work we did with good detail. You also tried to help us as much as possible.

—M

//

May 27, 2015

Mr. Fishkind, I believe that you are a good teacher and you taught us well this year. But sometimes, you had an attitude with certain kids for no reason, but overall, you were a good teacher.

—EM

===

May 27, 2015

I thought you were a good teacher overall. I had no problem with you except for the fact that we can't use our phones. But I thought you taught your lessons well. Sometimes I would need clarification. But for preparation, I give you a 10, for professionalism, I give you a 10 and for personality, I give you a 6...

—WM

//

May 27, 2015
Preparedness—5/5, Professionalism—5/5, Personality—4.5/5

You've have been an amazing teacher and I'm glad I've had the opportunity to be in your class. Your tough, but I know it's for my good and I appreciate that. I know people (especially in our class) disrespect you and don't appreciate you but keep teaching the way you do because there is always those handful of kids that appreciate you, including me! Thank you <3!

—EM

==

May 27, 2015

If I had to rate your performance Mr. Fishkind, I would rate you out of 10: Personality:9 Preparedness:10 Professionalism:10 you are amazing teacher and taught me self-discipline and to be a strong-minded person.

—AN

///

May 27, 2015

Your preparedness is very good. Your professionalism is ok when you tell us to be silent, you can be rude to some people, even if they are being rude themselves does not mean over past their rudeness other ways is alright. Your personality is decent because you can help and be funny at points, but not all the time.

—AO

==

May 27, 2015

In terms of preparedness, you have prepared extremely well for every assignment, and prepared us students for the upcoming test and EOC's required. You've remained professional while teaching us, but that doesn't prevent your fun and sarcastic personality form shining through. You've taught this class well and I'm so thankful to have such a unique teacher such as yourself.

—P

//

May 27, 2015
Readiness—10, Professionalism—10, Personality—TBD

I give you a 10 for readiness because you always know exactly what we need to do every day. I give you another 10 for professionalism. But for personality, it's hard because you get frustrated easily. But I understand why you get frustrated though because I would too.

—AR

===

May 27, 2015
Preparedness—1, Professionalism—10, Personality—10

I would rate your preparedness a 10 because we have something to do every day, whether it's work, or just the warm-up or reading. I would give you a 10 on professionalism.

—MR

//

May 27, 2015

While attending Everglades, I have had to deal with a lot of irresponsible teachers. I am grateful Mr. Fishkind wasn't one of them. He is always prepared, professional and responsible. I rate him a 10 out of 10, even on his bad days...

—AT

===

May 27, 2015

Preparedness—always at school on top of grading people's work on the same day with that gives plenty chances to bring up your grade. Never a day without work, everything is on his website if you're lost to do. Professionalism—knows what to do—always has an answer on many subjects. Personality—there's a lot about you because you have an interesting life also an understanding person and you get to know a student on a personal level.

—WV

//

May 27, 2015
Period 4—10/10

Because you have been one of the best teachers I have ever had. Also because of your intelligence and personality.

—CSA

===

May 27, 2015

Always stood on task when the class got out of control and always answered our questions. Plus, you're an awesome person over-all! We will miss you Mr. Fishkind >>>)):>

—CVA

///

May 27, 2015
10/10

Your preparedness has been great—every day you have plans for us. I don't recall one day you have not had plans for us. Your professionalism is great. When kids misbehave [*Cough, cough,* MV] you kept calm even though on the inside you were at your boiling point. You always kept your chill. Your personality is spot on. You are funny, smart and a good person. I wish I have you for another class next year!

—AB

==

May 27, 2015

In preparedness, Mr. Fishkind is always ready for class. In professionalism, you are always professional, even when people get rude. Sometimes you can be funny. This is my honest opinion.

—MB

///

May 27, 2015

You get an A-because the way you handled things were kind of wrong. But overall, I learned a lot and I can say you honestly cared. Thank you for the experience.

—KD

===

May 27, 2015

Mr. Fishkind was a good teacher. He prepared me very well for the start of the year. I wish I was in this class again so I can learn more and gain more knowledge.

—KH

//

May 27, 2015

I would say you are a very prepared teacher and you're good at teaching us all we need to know. I don't remember one time when you were not prepared for class. I don't think you've ever had a sub for this class either, which is really rare, compared to the other teachers in this school. You do the best job you can do. You constantly have to deal with kids interrupting and being rude and you still manage to get through a whole lesson every day. Personality wise, you're very respectful, even when kids aren't respecting you. You also are playful and make people laugh. You're also very educated and have taught me a lot this year. You are a very generous person, always letting me and others turn in assignments late, even when you say late work is not accepted. Keep up the same job next year!! ☺

—AJ

===

May 27, 2015

I give Mr. Fishkind a 10, just not because he's my favorite teacher, he's my friend, someone you I can trust, and also my sparring partner. He makes this subject easy and fun. He kind and a very easy person to work with it. I would love to have him next year also.

—EL

//

May 27, 2015

Well-organized. Challenging work. Likeable personality. Works hard and demands the very best from his students and is flexible til they gained their grade.

—JM

===

May 27, 2015

This year I think I had one of the best English teachers ever. He always gave us a challenge when it came to assignments. He knew when to fool around and when to take things seriously.

—AM

//

May 27, 2015

Preparedness: you were prepared very well in my opinion. You gave us work to prepare us for the grade ahead and test our ability. Not many teachers do that for us because they don't care. And that make you awesome.

Professionalism: I think you can handle a lot because you are so professional. Like certain people I won't name names, but you know who it is. I know there have been some time where you have wanted to give them the ol' one-two just as much as I have. And I respect you for that.

Personality: You have an awesome personality, because of that, I consider you one of the best teachers I've ever had. And I don't think it'll ever be less in my book...

—SN

===

May 27, 2015

Mr. Fishkind, I would rate you a 10 because you're a great teacher who offers understanding. You're experienced and your vocabulary is outstanding. You follow conduct, rules and order. You respect your students and teachers and co-workers. You always have ready lesson plans, and your prompts and assignments are realistic and fair. They challenge us to the best of our abilities w/o being too difficult to comprehend—and should we misunderstand, you're always there to fairly help and explain as much as you're able to. You're a very interactive and honest teacher. You're fair when circumstances change. You're positive and always prefer to help than to judge. Your support for your students gives them confidence and always for comfort. Thank you for being a great influence and instructor in my life.

You're highly appreciated. You are honestly the greatest teacher I've ever had. You have control and you do your job well. Thank you.

—R

///

May 27, 2015

Mr. Fishkind has been one of the best teachers I've ever had. In terms of preparedness, I give him a 10 and for professionalism I give him and 10 and for personality, he gets a 10 and I'm being 100% honest.

—CS

===

May 27, 2015

Mr. Fishkind is a great teacher! There was never a day where he wasn't prepared! He is quite professional, and never puts his personal feeling against a student. Mr. Fishkind is a really nice and cool guy.

Having a conversation with him is always fun. Education-wise, he is very good at teaching! Mr. Fishkind is definitely my favorite teacher this year!

—RU

///

May 27, 2015

Your performance was steady and good. You didn't take crap from students. And you made sure your students past your class with a 'C' or better.

—MV

===

May 27, 2015

Mr. Fishkind helped me grow as a learner and a person. He helped me grow as a person because he always seems to keep his cool. No matter how much people disrespect him, he just stays calm, and I think that's a really good characteristic. I think he did a really good job teaching. I just didn't do my part by putting in the time and effort into my work. But I still managed to get a 'B', so he did a really good job teaching.

—JW

///

May 27, 2015

I think that everything is prepared & organized in terms of preparedness. Grades were always in on time & you handle everything well-mannered as in professional. Personality-wise, I've never had a bad encounter with you so on a scale of 1–10, I'd give you a 10 as a whole this year.

—W

===

May 27, 2015
Period 3: Preparedness—10, Professionalism—10, Personality—9

Preparedness: 10—you're ahead of the game
Professionalism: 10—you take your job seriously
Personality: 9—you're an open book, but not enough pictures
You are a nice and helpful teacher. From all of my classes, you're
the one who knows what they're doing. Yeah, my other periods didn't
grade some of my work!

—JA

//

May 27, 2015
Preparedness—10, Professionalism—10, Personality—9

On preparedness, you had done well with what, why and where
because on the EOC, you had to answer what, why and where. I give
you a 10. On professional, you wear dress cloths to teach. You're the
only I know that do that. You also manage the grades and the classroom in a professional manner. I give you a 10. You are a little bit of
everything: a teacher, a musician and etc. you have the best personality out of my teachers—9.

—LA

===

May 27, 2015
Preparedness—10, Professionalism—7, Personality—5

I think that sometimes you annoy me, but you are always professional. You are also a good teacher.

—JA

//

May 27, 2015
Preparedness—10, Professionalism—10, Personality—10

I think you do an amazing job at teaching us & I'm glad that we actually do stuff in class, even if it's the last week of school.

—VA

===

May 27, 2015

Overall, I would rate you a 9 on everything. All year things have been very organized. Dealing with misbehavior has been done in a very fair manner. You have treated everyone with respect and equally.

—AA

//

May 27, 2015

On a scale of 1–10, I would rate Mr. Fishkind to be honest a 10, on professionalism, kindness, and inspirer. As an English teacher, Mr. Fishkind has taught me more than literature and schoolwork. He has taught me about life and patience. To be dealing with more than 100 students a day and still be patient and always have a smile on his face is just inspiring to me. I have 7 classes and out of the 7, my favorite teacher is Mr. Fishkind. I honestly couldn't have asked for a better teacher than him.

—AB

===

May 27, 2015
Preparedness—10, Professionalism—9, Personality—10

You always came to class prepared and ready to work. The work and the way the class is set up is very professional. Your personality is very cool and funny also at times.

—AC

///

May 27, 2015

In a scale of one to ten, I give my teacher, Mr. Fishkind, a seven. He is a great teacher and a great motivator. He's a smart and wise man but can have rules that don't benefit the students. The no phone rule is bad in my case because I work faster and high quality.

—JC

===

May 27, 2015
Preparedness—8, Professionalism—10, Personality—9

On preparedness, I will give you an 8 because whenever I was stuffy, you didn't have paper towels! But whenever I needed a pencil or paper, you offered it without a doubt. In professionalism, I give you a 10 because your vocabulary was quite impressive and you always knew the answer to every question, so your professional at heart! And you only didn't wear a button down maybe more than 3 times a year. And for your personality, I give you a 9, 'cause you always did tell funny jokes and whenever we were sad. You always showed you cared, which I appreciated very much, and I still do appreciate you have taught me so much about life on what to do and not to do.

—KC

///

May 27, 2015

Mr. Fishkind's performance is a 10. I know I have learned many things from him. His personality is very good he is funny and cool. I wish he can be my English teacher for the next years of my High School life.

—JG

==

May 27, 2015
(Just remember, these are the real deal and not all are rainbows and kittens…)

To be honest, you was cool from the beginning, then started going to then end of the year, you is getting aggrivated. You'll always say my name while someone doing the same thing I'm doing is talking. I'll rate you a 3 out of 10 you be annoying me somedays most likely every day.

—JW

///

May 27, 2015
Preparedness—10/10, Professionalism—9/10, Personality—9/10

I really enjoyed my time spent in Mr. Fishkind's class. And not from him telling us so much about him & his background story. Just as he was able to open up, so was I & I did that through my essays.

—AW

===

May 27, 2015
Period 7

Mr. Fishkind has done a good job with preparedness this year. Everything was organized. Professionalism has been good too. There weren't really that much problems except for the public speaking part. I didn't like how we had to speak in front of the class. But personality was good, I have no problem with that.

—CA

//

May 27, 2015
Preparedness—10, Professionalism—10, Personality—10

He was always prepared when teaching. Most professional & formal teacher I have. Personality is very helpful & relates to when teaching.

—KA

===

May 27, 2015
Preparedness—9, Professionalism—10, Personality —7

You were a great teacher obviously we're going to have conflict, but I've learned a lot.

—MC

//

May 27, 2015

I believe that my English teacher of my Sophomore year was very outgoing, brilliant, and professional towards educating his students. Academically, it has been a very important experience as a tasteful and active member of the English II force, and I believe that Mr. Fishkind was an important addition to expecting good morals and experience, especially from such an exuberant and proud man of stature and humor. I do appreciate his candor and sacrifice he has given unto us as his own.

—OD

==

May 27, 2015

To be very honest, you were very prepared with everything. You're a very great teacher. You're very professional with everything & your personality made this year a whole lot better & easier.

—DDR

//

May 27, 2015

I would rate your performance this year as a 6.5 out of 10. Constant presence was very good, as well as preparedness. I do think the system of discipline could have been dealt with differently. I also think more group work could've been done.

—NG

==

May 27, 2015
Preparedness—100%, Professionalism—97%, Personality—85%

Preparedness—100%: You were always prepared.
Professionalism—97%: You keep your class professional at times. Because
Personality—85%: Because you can be a complete you know what but being like that has made my writing better.

—DG

///

May 27, 2015

Our teacher has taught us value, meaning. When something was going on in the real world, he would make us write about how we felt about it. He is a good teacher and a great person. He has taught us everything we could know. From my point of view, I give my teacher a 10 because he deserved it. He gets us ready for the real world. He doesn't play, he takes things serious.

—JH

==

May 27, 2015
Preparedness—10/10, Professionalism—10/10, Personality—8/10

You was always ready for the next day. Always willing waste your time to reteach if we don't understand. Grades were always accurate. Have a nice and funny personality. You have very good patients [patience] with us. You've been a good teacher. Also, like all your ties!!

—MJP

//

May 27, 2015

We were on a very great teacher. I really loved this class. You were well-prepared for this school year. I guarantee other people feel this way as well.

—DK

==

May 27, 2015

I think you have done a really good job on your preparedness. You have taught this class so much and I know some people don't think so. You taught me a lot about writing and what you expect of me. I appreciate the comfort and how you believe in me. You guided me to success, and I think I will do great when I get older because of you. I give you a 10 out of 10.

—WL

//

May 27, 2015

Your performance, Mr. Fishkind, was great. You were understanding and knew how to handle every situation. You understand that it wasn't easy sometimes. You have a great personality, a rather funny one. And were a beast in basketball when I saw you playing in the gym. You were a great teacher, and I was happy to have you this past year. Thanks for the great. I also think you never missed a day this year.

—MM

==

May 27, 2015

Mr. Fishkind is one of the best teachers I have had all year. He doesn't miss anything when it comes to being prepared. Every day, we have a writing assignment and a schedule on the board. Being a teacher is a very hard job when you have a tough set of students. You have to be professional to keep your cool. I haven't heard him yell all year, so I think he has done a good job.

Mr. Fishkind is a pretty cool teacher and has a nice personality for a teacher. I give him a 9 out of 10. I would give him a 10, but he gives a LOT of work so…

—KN

//

May 27, 2015

I rate your performance an 8. You're always ready to read to the class and you have a lot of enthusiasm. You're always professional and prepared 24/7.

—TS

==

May 27, 2015

Preparedness: 10—always has something for us to do—we never have a 'free' day

Professionalism: 10—never absent, always teaching us something

Personality: 9—easy to talk to

—DT

//

May 27, 2015

You do very well prepared, professionally, such as reading books to us. We've been reading that other classes do not learn, as '1984'… Everything you say, we are very well prepared and highly effective. You are a person with a string personality, cheerful, sociable with everyone, or help others. You made it easy for students to understand many things.

Sometimes you get angry, but that only helps the structure better, less talking and working.

—DV

==

May 27, 2015

This school year with Mr. Fishkind has been okay. He is kind and nice but does have a temper. When he gets mad, he get mad. Most of the time, he is reasonable. He is good at teaching and not only English, but about life. He is a good person. I am glad that I got to spend this school year in his 7-period class.

—AV

//

May 27, 2015

Mr. Fishkind, I rate your performance 10 stars! You did an amazing job and I like that you don't yell and that you have a lot of patience. I know we make your job pretty hard, so I give you props for staying here and continuing your teaching career. Your personality is better than most of the teachers I deal with. Your professionalism and your very organized and you have prepared us for next year. ☺

—KZ

This last group was a pretty rowdy bunch. They gave me a run for my money about half the time. At one point, I had them write a punitive essay about class conduct. That pretty much ended all the non-sense, and they proceeded to work like the tenth graders they are. And now, we will hear from my creative writing students—end-of-year ratings for 2014–2015.

==

Period 6
Creative Writing

May 27, 2015

Preparedness—A+: always have an assignment ready.
Professionalism—B+: you can get into a conversation pretty quick…
Personality—A+: you're pretty funny.
Course grade—The Course is very intriguing, and the new topics every day keep me interested.

—SB

///

May 27, 2015
Preparedness—10/10, Professionalism—10/10, Personality—10/10, Course—9/10

First and foremost, I want to thank you. Instead of adhering to the stifling English standards and forcing your classes to write to a benchmark, you allowed individual thought. As you know, I'm a fan of language, and how beautifully manipulated it can be to portray an idea, however, Florida's education system neglects exploration of the English language. Instead of writing about whatever inspires students, schools force us to analyze and drown on and on about insignificant and stuffy literary pieces. Throughout this course, you have assigned several daily projects that broaden the horizon and require us to use reasoning and morals. Every day, you have approached us with a topic from the legalization of recreational marijuana to the anniversary of 9/11, and I, for one, was not aware of some of these issues until you mentioned them. To me, this course was also a class on current events, that encouraged lively debate and revealed several viewpoints. I think that this class has inspired me to activate the creative region of my brain and implement them into my basic English class. As far as your personality, you are truly the perfect instructor to teach this course. Your lively and relaxed spirit facilitated the creation of stellar literacy assignments. In addition, you are extremely supportive, and you constantly give out compliments on my work. I have truly enjoyed the class, and I thank you for having a little something for everyone.

—JB

===

May 27, 2015

I will say you get 10/10 when it comes to how prepared you are when it comes to giving us daily learning activities & writing prompts. You're always keeping it professional in class and treating all of us with respect. You're a teacher who has a unique, likeable and relatable teacher. I will say I do think you should be a little more strict when it comes to due dates. Many students, including me, take advantage over the face that we can turn in a writing assignment all the way to the end of the quarter.

—DC

//

May 27, 2015
Preparedness—10/10, Professionalism—10/10, Personality—10/10

He is always prepared and organized—doesn't misplace work & always has fun topics/currents events to write about. He is very professional, but I see him more as fun than professional. He is always jumping around and never dull—very funny & interactive.

—RE

==

May 27, 2015

Throughout this year, you have challenged our mental ability and creative ability. You pushed us to really think, not a lot of teachers do that. Having no boundaries made me feel like I can express myself however I want/wish to. Traditionally, students put teachers on this pedestal like they aren't human, or something. With you, I honestly felt like we were on the same level and we were just cool. I enjoyed this year, and I would like to thank you.

Love,
JJ

//

May 27, 2015
Preparedness—10/10, Professionalism—10/10, Personality—100/10

You are always prepared to explain a new topic to the class, and you are always organized about your work. I rated you a 10 because your very organized with the topics and work. You're a really cool teacher and very passionate about the things we write about. That is what makes you stand out from all the other teachers at the school.

—SJ

==

May 27, 2015

I really enjoyed taking this class this year, I feel that the topics were really easy to write about, with the exception of a few, which were really very challenging for me. I believe that this class is a great experience to be really creative. I also believe that you are a great teacher and explain things in a way that others can understand well. I appreciate the clarity and your manner of speaking. Thank you for making this class enjoyable.

—MM

///

May 27, 2015

I remember writing something just like this last year for English II for you. I feel like it was just yesterday. Your performance this year in Creative Writing has been absolutely amazing. I can truly tell you enjoy teaching this course so much. You look so much happier in this class then you ever did in English. I guess it's because you can truly express yourself in this class. You have made all of us such amazing writers with all those warm-ups. I have learned so much this year and I thank you for that. ☺

—VN

==

May 27, 2015

Pros: Topics are always fresh
Helps us with our writing skills
Professional and funny
Always prepared
Colorful personality

Beautiful mustache
10/10—Hair
Final grade—A+

—SP

//

May 27, 2015

Mr. Fishkind's performance was honestly beyond words. He was more than a teacher, but a mentor with countless experiences, axioms, idioms, and mottos for almost every situation. I wasn't expecting this when I switched into this class seeing last years' program was so subpar. He accommodated to all our requests and took our odd personalities which would usually scare others away, as endearing. Best of all, he doesn't judge over any circumstances, which is amazing. We had a mind-boggling prompt every day, which at times, stumped me. But Mr. Fishkind was there to help every part of the way. Course rating: 1000000000/10.

—JP

PS: This student came back to the school as part of the faculty in the school year 2019–2020.

==

May 27, 2015

You always have interesting assignments ready for us, which is good, and you do grade very quick, which is also great!

Professionally, the *Literary Magazine* looked nice. I do wish the classroom environment was a little more professional. I know that talking to others may be a good way to generate ideas, but it can also be distracting and create an environment that is hard to think in [there were forty-six students in my room for this section]. I know some people love it, but for me it more often causes distraction…especially when it gets really loud… The course itself is interesting, but there were times when I felt that some of the small one-day assignments were almost a little too easy…but there was also a good number of longer, more difficult assignments, so I guess it balanced out. I think that maybe you could change some of the assignments, because a good number of the assignments were current news events—and next year, there will be different current news events. I do feel like I learned some good things from this course—like, I learned what a vignette is, and I learned more about news this year than I would have otherwise. I learned from the assignments that made me think. And throughout the years, I got lots and lots of practice—very important to getting good at anything. I appreciate how open you are, and that you are willing to work with me individually when I need it.

—HR

///

May 27, 2015
Preparedness—5/5, Professionalism—5/5, Personality—5+/5, Course—5/5

You've been extremely prepared for class every day, evident of the fact that we always have something to write. I have seen you act very professional, especially with other teachers, but I also find it good that you can still relate to our age group, basically acting like a friend instead of a superior adult. I personally enjoy your personality taking up the room every day. Especially at the beginning of the year, what with you always playing music. It's also nice seeing you love writing and literature just as much as the rest of us, and that you understand what it's like to be a teenager in school. This class has by far been one of my favorites. I have time to catch up on other classes, but I've also been able to write more. The topics and types of literature that we've been writing have been particularly challenging and interesting as well. It's also been nice to see that so many editorial topics have been on current/important events, so that we keep up with the world and keep open minds.

—AR

===

May 27, 2015
10s everywhere

It was a great class to take, and nothing should be changed, all I have to say is good luck to the students next year!

—JS

///

May 27, 2015

Mr. Fishkind, you have been a nine. You have been extremely prepared with a prompt every day and have been very professional with your students in sixth period. You have the right personality for a teacher, not too strict, but not too kind. This course has been a great experience. I will probably be taking this course in Senior year. Thanks for an amazing sixth period this year.

—NV

===

May 27, 2015
Preparedness—5/5, Professionalism—5/5, Personality—5/5, Course—12000/5

Mr. Fishkind, I can honestly say you are one of my absolute favorite teachers, and I looked forward to your class every day. ☺ Your assignments never failed to make me think and explore the possibilities. Plus, you have a great sense of humor and are careful not to offend anyone. Overall, I think you're an amazingly awesome teacher—don't ever change anything!

—NV

//

May 27, 2015

As this year went by, the Creative Writing class I have been enrolled in has been wonderful, especially with my favorite teacher, Mr. Fishkind, Currently a Junior, headed to senior Year, I had Mr. Fishkind 2 years ago for English (English Honors I/Creative writing Period 6) and he made the class very enjoyable. His personality is quite nice, and he does his best to understand his students. He is quite professional when preparing work, or taking about upcoming deadlines, but he has made my first year in this course a remarkable experience, and I look forward to what the class will be next year. BEST TEACHER EVER!!

—XW

==

Period 5
Creative Writing

May 27, 2015
Preparedness—10, Professionalism—10, Personality—10

I thoroughly enjoyed this course and everything I was given the opportunity to write. I learned many new forms of poems, stories etc. and had a blast in this class. I also improved my writing, which is a relief to me. However, even though I loved this class, I think maybe a few more assignments pertaining to short stories would be enjoyable next year.

—DA

//

May 27, 2015

Preparedness: A—There was never a day when I came into this class and there was nothing assigned

Professionalism: A—Never unprofessional even when students disrespect you. /always calm and understanding.

Personality: A+—Very outgoing, funny and a joy to be around. Overall, one of my coolest teachers (and I don't have many of them)

Course: A—I enjoy the different topics we are assigned every day. I really like that they are topics that are modernized and relatable.

What can be improved? I personally think you are very learned. When it comes to the work, which makes people think they can take advantage of you. So maybe be a little more strict on the students, but don't go overboard.

—AB

==

May 27, 2015

I give you 100 all around Mr. Fishkind. No, I'm not trying to be a kiss ass because I truly believe you are ready to throw at us fun & games every day and you may be a goof and sarcastic, but you really do keep everything professional. This class is a blast to me and absolutely amazing. I don't believe there has been a day that you didn't readily have something for us to think about (excluding make-up days) you are hilarious and there is never a dull moment with you. I would absolutely love to come back next year.

—NC

///

May 27, 2015

Preparedness: Overall, Mr. Fishkind deserves 10/10 for pre-paredness. There has never been a day in his class where an assignment is not prepared for us to complete.

Professionalism: While Mr. Fishkind is extremely friendly, he is also very professional.

Throughout the year, he has shared stories with us of where his professionalism has allowed him to prevail in difficult situations.

Personality: the best part about Mr. Fishkind is his warm personality. In my three years of high school, he is one of the more understanding teachers I've had. He's told us of how much he's been through in life and still continues to have a great outlook and attitude in life. Very inspiring man.

Course: Creative writing has been a great outlet for writing my opinion on topics and expressing my feelings through the art of literature.

—JD

==

May 27, 2015

Preparedness: 10—very good
Professionalism: 10—very good
Personality: 10—cool

Every day you're prepared to have us working and busy. You come to school dressed accordingly and use cool language. Very fun to joke with. You're weird, in a good way, of course.

—ED

//

May 27, 2015

Your performance is good. I feel that our warm-ups are challenging as are the topics that we must think about and process, the reason why I always turn in my warm-ups late.

Preparedness, umm, I mean you always help me and tell me what's going on in the world because I haven't watched the news in three years and I never know what's going on. You are very professional. Rate: 10. Even after school, you will not talk wrong about anyone, and always try to teach, which is your job and you never, ever curse. You should actually get a reward for that. I feel like this class gets me ready for politics we write a lot about our feelings based on the laws and what we think is right and wrong about the government. I thought this class would help me in journalism, but it actually teaches me about life.

—NG

===

May 27, 2015
Preparedness—9, Professionalism—9, Personality—10
(Said I deserve all ten, but it would not seem authentic.)

Mr. Fishkind is honestly one of the best teachers I've ever had. He is always prepared for class and managed to keep a class of 50+ students. Senor Fishkind's professionalism exceeded necessary typical levels, that of other teachers. On top of all that, he has a great, witty personality and keeps me enthralled. The course was interesting and helped me open up.

—LJ

//

May 27, 2015
Preparedness—95/100, Professionalism—100/100,
Personality—100/100

No one call fully be prepared for a bunch of creative, loud-mouthed writers, however, 'twas a great attempt to summon us all.

Define professionalism: your teaching methods are on a whole different level. Of course, in a bizarre, great way. When professionalism is necessary, it excelled.

You are such a character. Your personality is beyond any expectation. Almost like golden flower blooming with words and literature.

—NM

===

May 27, 2015

Mr. Fishkind is the kindest teacher I have. He is always prepared with work and always welcomes all to class with a smile on his face. He understands people's needs and does not judge others. He is smart, hilarious, courteous and clever. He is a great person. He makes Creative Writing fun and original. I'm glad administration forced me to take this elective course. Rate: 20/10.

—MM

//

May 27, 2015
Professionalism—8, Preparedness—8

Mr. Fishkind has been one of the best teachers I've ever had. I've learned that there are NO LIMITS when it comes to Creative Writing. He's been a really nice person and I love how he's so outgoing. We have never had a day without an interesting concept.

Mr. Fishkind makes it so obvious that he is really passionate about English and Creative Writing. I feel like he is one of those teachers that teach because he actually likes it!

—DM

===

May 27, 2015
Preparedness—9.5/10, Professionalism—10/10,
Personality—100/10

Mr. Fishkind is the best literature teacher possible. He's fun, cool, calm, plays amazing music, a wonderful singer, and athletic (and a rad fish). He's very prepared (sometimes no, but most of the time, yes) 9.5 out of 10. Every day, he'll come up with a specific topic that deals with whatever happens during the month, week or even the day. Most of the time, they were challenging, but I was able to pull through. He's very professional, 10 out of 10 (deserves millions of dollars) knows how to handle situations, reminds students (even if work is due a month late) about late works, even gives advice to students about life, and how to handle it. I love it when he plays music (incredible on the guitar) on his laptop (80's and 90's music are my favorites—pina colada) Personality is flippin' wicked (wicked as in awesome) 100 out of 10. He's the nicest guy/teacher/friend there is: cool, calm, rad, athletic, smart, et cetera. Ever since the first day of school, I thought Mr. Fish was Albert Einstein, he's the reading kind of him, just got to add a bit of different ingredients. No one can replace him (he's one of a kind) Mr. Fish might not act serious, but he really is (just tries to hold that side and pin him down) Mr. Fish is also a big coffee lover and DC fan (Yes!!)
PS—hope you do well on become or have that career.
The course hast unlocked my talents. Writing stories was a very good/creative course I chose. It was difficult at first because I was under so much stress (stupid rules) but his class, man oh man, was a class that let my brain focus and relax simultaneously.

I hope they'll have a class like this in other schools, plus there should be more teachers who would want to teach creative writing.

—EN

//

May 27, 2015

Preparedness: Every day when I walked into class, you always had a topic ready for us to write about. Whether it was a topic or certain assignment, you always had something for us to do. To me, that's more than being prepared.

Professionalism: As far as I'm concerned, you had the perfect amount of professionalism for a teacher. The balance of maturity and sarcasm was on the dot.

Personality: One of my favorite male teachers—not too strict but not too lenient.

Course: I lover the course. Each topic/assignment was unique to itself. I liked how we wrote about current events but also wrote poems and plays. It was different than what I expected coming in, but that's a good thing.

—PO

==

May 27, 2015
Preparedness—9.5/10, Professionalism—9.5/10,
Personality—9.5/10

Mr. Fishkind has been a really great teacher and professor. Honestly, I have learned a lot during his class, and I feel like I have grown more as a writer. If I were to give a rating on preparedness, professionalism and personality, he would get a rating of 9.5/10 Honest opinion.

—AP

//

May 27, 2015

As a student in this amazing class, I believe you, Mr. Fish, is an amazing teacher, you perform your job with care and etc., but maybe more group projects & etc. should be done, but otherwise, this course is great!

—KP

===

May 27, 2015
Preparedness—10/10, Professionalism—10/10, Personality—10/10, Course—6/10

Never was there a day work wasn't prepared. You did treat every student as an individual & with respect, however, you let people take advantage of you too easily, so you could be a little more stern sometimes for the sake of staying professional. You're very kind and open-minded. You make this a fun class. This class allowed me to expand my mental, even though I didn't reach my full potential with a lot of assignments. You were a wonderful teacher who I will never forget. My only problem is the amount of students & somedays not being able to find a seat. It's also to many energies to take in. The people are very loud & I'm a very "chill" person, so the volume was overwhelming some days.

—RQ

//

May 27, 2015
Preparedness—10, Professionalism—8, Personality—10, Course—9

Always had the assignments ready and on the board. You were professional and not strict (which is a good thing). You also told the right amount of jokes.

You were filled with life and held good conversation. I liked how I was forced to be creative, however, more group work would be better.

—AR

==

May 27, 2015
Preparedness—8/10,   Professionalism—9/10,
Personality—90000000/10, Course—Infinity

Mr. Fishkind exhibits very ordered and prepared traits in his behavior. He has only forgotten/not had time to write the prompts on the board a maximum of 4 times. He is a hard-working teacher. Also, a lightning-fast grader. Mr. Fishkind is a very jovial person but does not let his personality interfere with his professionalism. He spilled coffee on my paper once, but I can easily rewrite it. Mr. Fishkind had been a great teacher. He gives wonderful commentary and advice. I have learned much from him in my time here. He has helped me reawaken my long dormant passion for writing and I will have a very tough time saying goodbye to him next week.

—SS

//

May 27, 2015

Preparedness: I think you were always ready to teach the class, despite the fact that we are a loud group of kids. You always had our assignment written and ready on the board. Also, you are always teaching us, or at least me, something new in the class.

Professionalism: I've never really seen you work professionally, but as a teacher, I feel like a teacher like you should get paid more because you teach kids to expand their creative minds.

Personality: You are one of my favorite teachers because I think you have a happy personality compared to some of the stricter teachers. I know you have your limit, though.

Course: On a scale of one to ten, I would say infinity. This class has really taught me to expand my thinking.

—BS

===

May 27, 2015
Preparedness—10/10, Professionalism—10/10, Personality—100/10

I feel like the course revolved around the warm-ups. There should have been more long-term projects and opportunities to do our own things instead of daily prompts, which ended up becoming mostly busy work. This is actually what I did in the course due to my frequent visits to the learning lab. Thanks for a great year.

—JT

_____

And finally, these are the letters I received, mainly from Graduating Seniors who had been my students in years past that I had a positive influence on—enjoy!

///

May 2015

So, it looks like we meet again Fishkind (this time with an actual graded assignment). But with all jokes aside I just wanted to say thank you for making this year one of my most memorable in high school. As much as we joke around about my laziness it was that character trait exactly, that made me sign up for the class. I figured since I took AP Language the year before that Creative Writing would be an easy 'A'. Despite being **OBVIOUSLY** wrong I have no regrets taking your class (but I do regret not taking your advice) and I would do it again in a heartbeat. Your class also came with a newfound appreciation of authors of all genres, but that's beside the point. I've learned more in your 5-minute introduction of the prompt than I have in any of my history classes, and it was your class that taught me the importance of deadlines (weather I met them or not). Aside from being a teacher you were also a guidance counselor you gave "the seniors" advice ranging from college applications to what to do if your friend is a major snoop. I'll definitely be back to visit you. It's only a matter of time before you see me and everyone else again. So, with that being said I guess I'll see you around, sincerely.

—AI

==

May 2015

This probably goes without saying, but I am very glad that I got you as a teacher. Thank you so much for all your help this year. Because you allowed me to take the time to do my own work, my writing has improved by leaps and bounds this year, as evidenced by the awards I won. I have also been more productive than ever before. Aside from that, you are a very cool dude, and I am glad I got to meet you. Have a great summer!

PS: This student has since gone on to become a journalist.

//

May 2015

Dear Mr. David Fishkind,

When my Sophomore year began you were not my teacher in the beginning but through the randomness of school, I ended up gaining you as my lasting English teacher. It always comes to chance that I get to experience subjects taught by marvelous educators, and you were most definitely one of the best chances I was given. I could not find such hospitality anywhere else but in your classroom. When I passed through your door, I could not help but feel a sense of equality and bliss. You showed me so much kindness that I almost felt unworthy, but in the end, I savored every iota of it. Openness radiated from you as you told your engaging stories and tales that have encompassed your life.

I never grew bored when listening to your speeches and I can always remember the zeal that came with you when you spoke. A student could not be more impressed as I was with you. I almost felt like you were a king among commoners, that a man of such conviction could bear the title of teacher. However, I thought to myself and came to the conclusion that that title fitted you to perfection. I will always strive to emulate your mannerisms and mutual respect you had for all of your students.

I could hear you now as I walk to the very end of the portables, "Having a good day, Mr. Yoham?" and seeing that unmistakable head of hair that you had made me smile because I knew I was going to a place where I could be comfortable and relieved of the stress of everyday school life.

I feel ashamed that I did not go into your Creative Writing class because I know I would have enjoyed every minute of it. Having you as my English teacher could not compare to having you as a Creative Writing teacher, we would be devoid of the standard books forced upon us in regular English classes and finally be able to embark into the depths of creativity and imagination. An impassioned teacher in a free writing class would be more than I could have asked for, but sadly, duty called me to engage in classes that were obligatory, and I could not say no.

I truly hope I get to see you at my Graduation. It would be a pleasure having you there as I walk across the stage and gain the diploma that I could have never gained without teachers such as yourself guiding me towards that achievement. I hope that I may gain the carefree spirit that you have shown me in one of the classes that I will surely never forget.

Sincerely,
JY

PS: I will also never forget seeing you at the P!nk concert while walking down the stairs.

The school year 2014–2015 represented a breakthrough for me as I got to teach an elective course, for which there was no established curriculum, so I wrote one. This was the first year I taught Creative Writing, which also involved gathering material for the *Literary Magazine* and running the Literary Fair, along with submitting material to the district. It was both rewarding and exhausting! Now on to 2015–2016, which will again feature English 2 regular students, along with creative writing students (who represent all four grades—9 to 12)! Enjoy!

==

Period 1

May 25, 2016

10 out of 10 and 10 is the best. You're always prepared, there is never a day that you didn't know what to do or say. You are very professional and good at what you do. You're not like these other teachers; you care about education more than just a percentage of the class that tells us. Your personality is very nice. You're the most caring teacher I have ever met. You give kids so many chances to turn in old work. You're also very funny. Overall, I'm glad I had you last year and this year again. Keep doing what you're doing, which is an amazing job.

—VA

///

May 25, 2016
Preparedness—10, Professionalism—10, Personality—10

You prepared all of us really well and every time we were taking a test, I felt more confident than ever. You handle your job very well. Every time someone gives attitude or anything you just acted professional about it. Out of all my teachers, with personality, you are my favorite one. I like when you talk to me in the middle of doing work and tell me stories sometimes. Also, when I used to leave my bag in your class, and you would tell me to have a good game or practice.

I just want to say thank you for everything. You really helped me a lot. Last year, I could barely get a 'B' in my English class and now I got all 'A's' in the 4 quarters. I really was fortunate to have you this year and I wish I could have you next year, too. I see no flaws on your teaching. Just keep teaching how you're teaching and whoever doesn't take advantage of your teaching ability is missing out.

—AB

===

May 25, 2016

To be honest, in the beginning of the year, I thought you were a little weird and annoying with all the work we got, but as the year continued, I realized how much you care for your job and for your students. I understand that you're passionate about what you do, and I appreciate everything you've done for me as a teacher, and you are in my top 3 favorite teachers and I'm quite glad I stayed. Rate 10.9

—L

///

May 25, 2016

Mr. Fishkind, all around, you're a great teacher. You're a smart and cool teacher. You have a great personality, very outgoing, and you love to be sarcastic and make jokes. Mr. Fishkind stays at his own character, he never switches up, even if something was to happen. Mr. Fishkind is very professional. He stays on top of all things he do in class. Your performance is always great. You project your voice, and if reading, you read clearly so everyone can hear. I disagree or dislike the music he play, he could at least put on jazz music. You can become better as an educator if you make things fun. The students will become very bored. No disrespect, but you're like an old-fashioned teacher, you only give work and work and work, and we can't keep up with that much work with 7 classes a day. Out of everything, you rate as a teacher 9.5 out of 10.

—A

==

May 25, 2016
Preparedness—10, Professionalism—10, Personality—10

You are a great teacher; your ways of teaching are very efficient when it comes to work. It's mostly our fault.

—DD

//

May 25, 2016

Mr. Fishkind performance this year was a ten. He did what a teacher is suppose to do; get us prepared for the Writing EOC and build our minds up. Mr. Fishkind personality was very unique; he had his own sense of humor and tasted in music. He's very kind and generous. When he sees something in someone, he don't give up.

These two years I spent with him went by fast, but everything was so worth it. I have improved my writing and learned over the course.

—TE

==

May 25, 2016

I would give Mr. Fishkind 9 rating for all around preparedness, professionalism and personality. Mr. Fishkind did a lot this year so I don't think there would be anyway else to become a better teacher.

—JE

May 25, 2016

To be completely honest, so far in High School, you have been my favorite teacher. To me, you have been a 10-10. Unlike other teachers, you treat us with respect and also like friends. There is nothing I think you should improve on honestly.

—SG

===

May 25, 2016

My performance this year was a 7 which is good compared to my previous year. This year, I actually tried on my work and studied in ways that would help me succeed. I have become a more social person rather than not talking to anyone. I used to be really lazy and not show up to school, but this year I pushed myself to get up and go to school.

My academic performance has improved a lot because of the people I started surrounding myself with and my goal to be a good student.

—SJ

Obviously, this student missed the prompt, which asked them to rate *my* performance, not their own, but for the sake of honesty, I have shared with you exactly what as written.

//

May 25, 2016

Well, what can I say right now? I am speechless. I don't think words can explain Mr. Fishkind as a teacher. I don't think you should be here teaching. I think you should be a million a year right now because of your personality, professionalism and preparedness. Well, your personality is excellent because in times when I am feeling down in class, he talked to me. When you tell us how to write an essay, you break it down in a way we can understand. You are never late to class, not ever. 10-10 best teacher ever.

—VM

==

May 25, 2016

Mr. Fishkind is a really good teacher. He's cool, intelligent and funny at the same time. He's always prepared with work for us to do. He's also professional as well. Whenever a student disrespect him he never gets out of character whit them. His personality is very rare. There's not a lot of people like him anymore.

The only thing I don't like about him or disagree with is his taste in music. It gives most people a headache and aggravates them. Overall, Mr. Fishkind is a 9 out of 10 teacher.

—EO

//

May 25, 2016

If I had to rate Mr. Fishkind's performance I'd give him a 10. Preparedness, professionalism and personality would be a 10. Maybe even 11. Everything is always on an exact point and is generous with work and in general. He helps us understand our work and can still be a fun/entertaining teacher.

—EP

==

May 25, 2016

If I was to rate the performance of Mr. Fishkind, I would rate him in scale of 1 through 10 I would give him a 10 because he helped me in passing my exams and writing better essays in class. He is a very good and very sarcastic man and funny. It was very fun being in his class.

—AR

//

May 25, 2016
Personality—10, Patience—15, Time management—10, Professionalism—10

Honestly, when I walked in your class on the first day of school, I thought I wasn't going to like you. You honestly grew on me. I would like to thank you for always caring for me and my grade even when I didn't care that much about grade during the 3rd quarter. Even though I didn't show it, I really did like your class and all the advice you gave me. I will miss this class. Thank you for everything! Hope you have a great summer!

—VR

==

May 25, 2016
Preparedness—10, Professionalism—10, Personality—10

You have really no flaws you are able to teach very well. You have some flaws like your music choice sometimes I like them other times no. I find you funny and cool and wish I didn't have to leave. I love your class. I also like your work edicate [ethic I think] and your organization. Not to lie I thought you was trying to scare us with your speech about how much work we were going to do. I also thought you was going to be a mean teacher because it is early in the morning for you to have to deal with us.

—DR

//

May 25, 2016

Mr. Fishkind teacher of English 2 in this year was excellent in the area of preparedness, his personality is very good because he helps students to get better grades and can understand what he is reading or explaining, and his professionalism, I think is also at the best teachers in the school because he explain the topic and his central idea is that one to the students understand what is explaining in that moment. I give him a 10 in all the aspects.

—WT

===

May 25, 2016

You said to be honest so I will be…
Personality: 10, time management: 10, mustache: 5, patience: 11, music: 2. [You can't always get what you want.]

Dear Mr. Fishkind,
I will lowkey miss your class as I get older. I came to realize that teachers care more for their money than the pass rates or the minds of their students. I'm so glad to be your student. Thanks for caring about my success as much as I did.

—TW

May 25, 2016
Preparedness—10, Professionalism—8, Personality—10

He is well-prepared throughout the day and when we walk in the work is already up on the board. He is a good educator but sometimes he can't be able to pronounce the word correctly. (I do have a speech impediment which is a hurdle for an English teacher.) He has a great sense of teaching. He can explain what type of work we can do or how to do it.

—DY

===

Period 3

May 25, 2016

I rate you at a 10 because you taught me the way I understood. I now have better vocabulary for when I am speaking. You taught me professionally and I learned so much more than in any other grade. You to me are fair, very fun and funny. You are the best English teacher in the whole time I have had an English teacher.

—DA

May 25, 2016

I personally rate you for overall performance task and teaching a 9 out of 10. Reason being is I feel as though you're a very good and attentive teacher. You're very responsible when it comes to putting in grades right away which is appreciated. I think you can improve when it comes to students asking you questions you need to listen a little more before going straight into answering. That is the only critic I have other than that you're a very fair and organized/responsible teacher. I've actually learned a lot thank you.

—AA

===

May 25, 2016

This school year I would rate you a 7. You have been a good teacher. You sometimes get mad at me for no reason. You love giving me Ds. I don't know why, and I do all of my assignments. You have a good personality overall. I really don't think we needed to do so much work this school year. I also didn't think I deserved Ds every quarter.

—TC

_____

And this just shows that you cannot please everybody, and some people just get Ds.

//

May 25, 2016
Preparedness—9, Professionalism—10, Personality—9

You had your highs and lows, but everybody does. You explained a lot of things on great detail, which was helpful. And I know if we had trouble in or out of school, we could talk to you. I believe you were my best teacher this year.

—BC

===

May 25, 2016

This year, I really enjoyed my Sophomore year. Like all my classes and teachers were really cool. I had high expectations when I first walked into school this year, I told myself I would do better than I did last year. However, I didn't like the fact that I had reading this year once again. Only because I've had reading since the 6th grade and all my other friends don't. I had Reading 3rd Period this year and my teacher was Mr. Fishkind. At first, he seemed cool like his personality was cool and weird and I liked it.

—KH

//

May 26, 2015

This year has been a great year for me. I loved all of my teachers and it has been a fun year for me. My teachers were fun and nice this year. Can't wait for next year and meet new people. Your performance this year was fine. You did give a lot of work and such a little time. You prepared us very good, and your professionalism was good too and your performance.

—PH

===

May 25, 2016

My performance this year was ok. But not ok it was just going up and down with everything in school but some thing I did get a good grad in my English class and my other class for this school year. But will do better next year.

—II

And another example of a student who missed
the prompt—at least they were honest...

May 25, 2016

Your performance over the year has been perfect. I learned and don't hate talking in public as much as at the beginning. You are always prepared and appear professional. I would rate your personality as a 9/10, one thing you could work on is getting people on track instead of never paying attention, but apart from that, you are always really helpful and nice.

Nothing really bad. The only way you can become better would be by controlling the noise level and attentiveness of the class in general. Everything else is good.

—AL

==

May 25, 2016

In my opinion, you have a 10 in preparedness. You are always ready for us as soon as we come in. You are always professional every day, never step out of line so I would rate that a 10. When it comes to personality, I would also rate a 10. From what I see and experience in this classroom I would only change one thing…GROUPS! I hate being on groups! I love working alone. In rows!

—CM

//

May 25, 2016
Preparedness—10, Professionalism—10, Personality—10

One thing about you Mr. Fishkind is that you're always prepared. You always have the assignments ready for the week. You always know what projects are going to take place in the quarter and because of your preparation ahead of time, it allows me to prepare and not procrastinate on the assignment.

You are one of the most professional teachers I have ever had. You don't miss class (I missed 4 days in 17 years) which is hard for anyone to do. You rarely let any students' behavior get to you, which is rare in teachers.

You are not only a good teacher, but also a great person.

You are very flexible when it comes to assignments and make up quizzes for people. You take time out of your own day to help them get their grades. I don't think you should change anything. Keep instructing the way you do.

—BM

===

May 25, 2016

Your performance this year was good. I didn't have any problems at all learning the material. You explained and demonstrated everything that was needed. You prepared us correctly. Everything was professional and your personality was good to. I'd say you would get 9 for preparedness, for professionalism. And 8 for personality.

—DN

//

May 25, 2016

Over the course of the school year, you have proven yourself to be one of the top educators in the school. You have taught us all we need to know and more. The SOAPSTONE, Dante, countdown and SIFT chart have taught a lot and I may show attitude be rude, but I like you as a teacher and your personality is very genuine and sincere. You are a great person as well teacher. Thank you. Rate: 9.8/10.

—MS

This student and I butted heads on a regular basis, but
in the end, respect was earned after it was given.

==

May 25, 2016

This year I have been actually able to increase my thinking capacity. In regard to preparedness, there is nothing but positive about it to
be said. Such as: you are always ready with something new. For everyone, everyday so that we can be able to increase our knowledge. If it
does not help us in any way, then you will not give it to us, which is a
good thing. Very organized and you always let us know what to do and
of we don't understand, you don't have to think twice about saying it
again, you just do. You don't have to change anything about yourself
as a teacher. You are a very outstanding individual and not only in the
teaching world. Coming to this class tells me that I am going to learn
something or do some type of work that will increase my knowledge. If
here is anyone that does not take your class seriously, they are missing
out. Let's just say that you just keep doing what you are doing because
it tends to make students like me, have a better perspective on life.

—HV

//

May 25, 2016

I would rate your performance this year an 8. I say this because
yes you did prepare us very well for next year, but I feel as if we
really as a class didn't connect with your personality. [Check other
responses—sounds like it is this student.] Also, at times you gave us
assignments but then added 5-4-3-2-1+1 which I never had enough
time to finish, making me have to hand it in late. It's like the work
was just too much for one day.

Other than that, I think you prepared us well and very professional.

—DW

Period 4
2015–2016

May 25, 2016

You are a good teacher. I guess you are very prepared and always prepared. You are very professional and take your job very SERIOUS! And I rate your performance 8. I rate your preparedness 9, and your personality is 6.

—CA

Six? Really? Guess they did not really like me after all…cannot please everybody…*sigh*

///

May 25, 2016

Fishkind my 2nd year with you I rate you 10/10. My favorite teacher who is very laid back and easy teaching.

—IA

===

May 25, 2016
Preparedness—10, Professionalism—9, Personality—8

Every day when we walk in our work is on the board. Every day we do work there is never a day when we don't have work.

You are very professional, but sometimes you take your job too seriously.

Some days you are cool, but most of the time you are very strict. Loosen up a little, live more stress less. Maybe take a couple of days off.

—SB

I love when they want to give me advice...☺

//

May 25, 2016

Mr. Fishkind you rate form me is an 8 ½ because even though we went through ups and downs your still a great instructor and educator even though you give a ton of work. I know and we know it's only for the better for us and for us to get smarter.

—BB

===

May 25, 2016

In all honesty, I feel you've done better than a "10 out of 10" Mr. Fishkind. You're an amazing English and Creative Writing teacher and so far, my favorite English teacher. It's not just how you teach, but your personality and attitude are spectacular. I'll always remember your trademark sarcasm. You've taught me a bunch, and not just English skills or creativity, but on how to become the man I will become ion the future. You've inspired me so much. In the beginning of the school year, I didn't really give my hardest, and I felt bad when I half-assed your assignments. I don't think I've ever had a closer relationship with any other teacher until now. Although you had your moments, it doesn't really, I can say that my closest sophomore teachery matter as everyone has those moments including myself through these near 9 months. I can say that my closest

Sophomore teacher was you. And just know when I'm a Senior, I'll be thanking you and visiting you to say 'hello' very often. So, I guess my final grade for you is one hundred out of ten per sent, even if that's practically impossible, but you've showed me that anything can become possible, just from witnessing your life and struggles. Thank you, Mr. Fishkind. I appreciate everything you've done.

—GC

///

May 25, 2016
Preparedness—9, Professionalism—10, Personality—6

You're always prepared, the board always has classwork ready.
You are very professional.
You're a little too serious. You never laugh and your very sarcastic.

—EC

==

May 25, 2016

From 1–10 I'll give an 8 because your professional, prepared & ready for the day, and taught me well this year. At times, your sarcastic which can be funny at times. You'd be an even better teacher if you didn't give a lot of work or homework over the weekend, but it got me better in my writing skills, so I guess it worked out well.

—JE

///

May 25, 2016

Mr. Fishkind is a great teacher he keeps you motivated and busy. Mr. Fishkind and I have had some rough times [I caught this student cheating on my midterm exam, along with two others.] but we worked through them. I remember at the beginning of the school year when I slept in his class and he didn't allow it. But to end this I just want to say that I like Mr. Fishkind because is very encouraging and he gives many chances so that you can pass the class.

—TF

==

May 25, 2016

I say on our preparedness all around you get a 7. You get a 7 not only because you but because of my fellow students. I based your rating on how fast you could give and get though an assignment. You gave us good assignments points to you but because my classmates not doing an assignment held us back, I took points from you. So, don't kick yourself to much about it. Your professionalism I give you about 10 out of 10 because your quick and to the point. Whenever we would make a speech, you would count down making it seem that I'm not talking to just a couple of students but many members of society. You always gave us chances to live or die kinda like a boss and kept things up but had control just as a boss would. Personality wise I give you another 10 out of 10. You made us laugh and understood what you were saying. I mean sometimes I didn't understand your jokes because they were a little to advance for me. Your very serious natured person sometimes I didn't understand your jokes because they were a little to advance for me.

Your very serious natured person sometimes I wouldn't know if it was appropriate to laugh or smile at something you said. After a while I could understand what was appropriate or not after a while. You also get points for being able to understand me and not judge me as a person.

—JF

May 25, 2016

Sometimes you skip me when I have to use the bathroom. But that doesn't matter. I don't care, water under the bridge. But other than that, you were goo, almost perfect. You were strict but fair, fun but not too fun.

—KH

May 25, 2016

In all honesty, you are the best teacher I never had before we have problems and you always there to help us to resolve then for my you have 100%.

—GI

May 25, 2016

Fishkind is the kind of teacher I could talk to when I need help with a problem. I appreciate everything he has done, and he really taught me a lot and it me feel like I should take an AP Literature class. I really hope Mr. Fishkind keeps it up and I'll remember him as my favorite teacher of my Sophomore year.

—FI

==

May 25, 2016

In this school year you have done 7 out of 10 because you have prepared us to test, quiz and other works. For some of the quiz make the question less confusing and your professionalism it can get good.

Your personality is great as a teacher and how you treat other student.

—DL

///

May 25, 2016
Preparedness—10, Professionalism—11, Personality—11

Mr. Fishkind well prepare his classes. It this class always organized for his next lesson. Mr. Fishkind a professional he should be a college professor English. Mr. Fishkind personality it great. I'm glad I met a teacher help it student to pass the 10th grade.

—DM

==

May 25, 2016

Mr. Fishkind is a great teacher he keeps you motivated and busy. Mr. Fishkind and I have had some rough times, but we walked through them [this student also was caught cheating on the midterm exam]. I remember in the beginning of the year when I slept in his class and he didn't allow it. Me and Mr. Fishkind probably started out on the wrong foot, but we finally made it to the finish line. Mr. Fishkind is very helpful and understanding and I respect that about him. Y'all put some respeck on his name.

—CM

//

May 25, 2016

In my full opinion I rate you a 10 out of 10. You are an amazing teacher, you are never late or tardy, you want the best for us & want us to succeed in life! Not most teachers care but you do care. You give us work that we think we can't do but you know we can, so you assign it & we get it done. So, from the bottom of my heart I thank you so much for making me semi-successful. I've learned so much from you. And I like how you are always there for us. And when I become big in the future, I'll shout you out with a thank you.

—BR

==

May 25, 2016

I think that you did a great job at teaching us and helping us understand stories that we did not understand and words that were difficult and we wrote a lot of essays that helped us understand the stories we read and some essays we wrote about our goals and what we had to do to get there.

—TR

//

May 25, 2016

Having Mr. Fishkind as my English teachers for my Sophomore year was a great experience. Mr. Fishkind is a good teacher; he teaches well, and he is very disciplined and strict even though we started off the year rough after he called my parents and they yelled at me. [This was the third student involved in cheating on the midterm exam.] I have straightened up. I became more serious. I reduced the way I talk and laugh and began to do my work. I have Mr. Fishkind as a teacher, and I think his class was a good experience. He's a great teacher who doesn't like to see his students fail. I like the fact that he gives us extra time to do the work that we missed. I like Mr. Fishkind, in fact, he's my favorite teacher. I would love to have him as a class teacher again.

—S

===

May 25, 2016

From my time in this English class, I think you are responsible, and you are organized with your work. You take pride in your profession and you are never disrespectful. You try to pass everyone, but only if they try to pass themselves.

—KT

//

May 25, 2016

In terms of preparedness, professionalism and personality, I would rate your performance from 1–10 and I rate a 10. From the first day to know you gave us work to prepare us for the FSA writing and for next year. Also, you play the music to make us get a visual view of what we are writing about helped me a lot to write better than I did last year. You had everything prepared for us the day before, helping me find out that being prepare dis more helpful than doing it. Personality is good, you talk to us like we are adults, and you respect each and everyone.

—VV

==

Period 5
2015–2016

Note: this was a rowdy bunch of under-performers with good students mixed in as well—they were a challenging group on a good day.

May 25, 2016

This year I had a lot of fun making new friends. This year I would say the same thing as last year. You were more fair with grades and make-ups. The only bad thing was the environment because nobody would be able to concentrate with all the noise that was made. Overall, everything else was great.

—JA

//

May 25, 2016

Overall, the 2016 school year, I personally think I learned a lot in this class and learned many techniques such as: 5-4-3-2-1 and the Dante's chart. A 10 best fits your personality, preparedness and professionalism for the following school, I hope it's a repeat of this year English because I've earned various of technique with the help of your personality, professionalism and preparedness.

—LB

==

May 25, 2016

My experience with Mr. Fishkind was good. He was a good teacher and was reasonable with all the kids. His teaching was good because he took his time to teach us, so I learned everything. Fishkind was a professional teacher.

His vibe was rant so he is a good teacher I like him.

—JC

//

May 25, 2016

I have only nice things about your performance this year. Having you for two classes gave me the chance to be instructed by you in both creative and strict environments. Considering the behavior you had to endure [even the other kids noticed] from each of those classes I think you handled yourself quite nicely. I'd hope to have you as a teacher every year of I could.

—JD

===

May 25, 2016

In terms of preparedness, professionalism and personality, I would rate your performance this year as a 10. You're a great educator, but if a student is causing trouble or being disrespectful [daily in this class—a *lot* of characters), you should try to find the root to their disturbance and disrespect. [Sigmund Freud would have needed a shrink after dealing with this group.]

—BG

//

May 25, 2016

Overall, this year your preparedness was a 10. Your professionalism, from a scale of 1–10 is 11 because of things that happened in class and you did not spazz out [*lol!*] or act out of character, but I do think instead of arguing and letting them disrespect you, you should just kick them out. Personality is a 10 because you've always amused us in a very educated way.

—CL

==

May 25, 2016
Preparedness—1, Professionalism—10, Personality—10

Mr. Fishkind your performance this year has been very outstanding. Your teaching methods has made work easy and understandable.
Your always prepared.
Your always organized.
Your personality is delightful.
Although people in class can be very disruptive, you're always prepared to handle them. You've been teaching for years so none of these behaviors are new to you, and you gradually learn how to deal with it. Most of the time, your always happy unless someone gets on your last nerves. You're a very intelligent man.

—TM

///

May 25, 2016
Preparedness—A+, Professionalism—A+, Personality—A+

Fishie 4 life.
I always wanted something to do every day, you always got us busy and that's been prepare for everything. Thanks. You never chock someone on this period, and that's very professional of you. You always try to be calm and keep going with the work. Thank to for gave me the dictionary. Your personality for one is very fish "kind". And also funny with obviously when the 'special' people

aren't around, and I like your absent "carraspera" It's short but it's honest and from the heart.

—VM

===

May 25, 2016
Preparedness—10, Professionalism—10, Personality—10

Always ready to teach and have work ready for us.
Honest and strict when it comes to grades and behavior.
Smart, funny, but still knows how to take school seriously.

Being the best teacher, I have had this year, I have nothing but good things to say about Fishkind. His performance overall was honest, organized and downright outstanding. His personality is very likeable. He knows how to joke around, make others laugh, etc. He is well-organized and strict when it comes to work.

I cannot really add anything to help him become better as an educator since he is a fantastic teacher!

—LP

//

May 25, 2016

This year there was ups and downs with me and you, but you saw the good in me but that goes for professionalism. You always have paper and pens for students to use and you always update your website unlike a lot of teachers. Your always prepared but you let kids get to you to easily your personality is the best thing about you. Overall rate: 8/10.

—RP

===

May 25, 2016

Since this is not my first time having you as an instructor, I'm already used to your unique and bold personality. Having you as an English teacher, it's been way different than being in Creative Writing and having more freedom. Your preparedness was well, and you prepared us well for the work and the test we needed to take, but I feel like instead of doing charts all the time, you could change up your assignments.

—BS

///

May 25, 2016

My experience with Mr. Fishkind this year was a good successful year. I feel as he prepared us well for the writing and reading FSA and also mentally prepared us for the pressure. He is a very professional teacher, one of the most in the school. The only thing that might need to change is his personality. I don't mind me but some kids in the class don't seem to like the way he approaches things. This feature really does not mind me though.

—CW

===

Notes on this period—I am not sure if you noticed that only twelve of the twenty-five students in this class even bothered to do this assignment/ evaluation. It should tell you much that even when essentially allowed to free-write their feelings, that they declined on a wholesale level.

And now on to...

//

Period 6
Creative Writing (2015–2016)

June 1, 2016
Preparedness—10, Professionalism—9, Personality—9

Preparedness—definitely a ten. You always have an assignment ready for us, every day, even if you have up late, there is something on the board.

Professionalism—I would give you a very strong 9, honestly, you're a teacher to us, but also a friend when we need it. Also, you would definitely handle yourself well in a more professional situation.

Personality—I would have to give you a nine, just because I think you're incredibly kind, but it can be taken for granted sometimes. It sounds bad, but it's just about you having a golden heart.

—HB

===

June 1, 2016
Preparedness—10, Professionalism—7, Personality—10

Before class, your assignment is coursed and ready to be announced. Sometimes you make jokes that normal teachers wouldn't, that's why your personality is a 10. Funny, interact with all students. Keep calm when class goes crazy. Stories to tell are great and personal projects you express to us.

—CB

//

June 1, 2016
Preparedness—9.7, Professionalism—10, Personality—10

You are, by far in my High School experience the best teacher I have ever had. I may not exactly show my enthusiasm, but I love coming to this class, I can't wait for the next school year.

—GC

===

June 1, 2016

10/10, don't have anything bad to say. Pretty nice and fair with all his students. The class is amazing, it's really cool to see how much different things we've written throughout the year.

It's also cool to learn about all the different types of writing. The class is very nice and laid back. It's nice to have a class you don't have to stress about.

—AC

//

June 1, 2016
Preparedness—9 (No one is perfect.), Professionalism—9 (Because no one is perfect.), Personality—10

I've thoroughly enjoyed your class and every moment that accompanies it. Thank you for the conversations and the lovely jokes and memories. Thank you so very much!

—NM

==

June 1, 2016
Preparedness—10, Professionalism—10, Personality—10

There's always a new topic for us to write about and discuss in class.

Mr. Fishkind never misses a class and is never immature, etc.

There's never a dull moment! Mr. Fishkind is funny, knowledgeable on Literature and History, and very open-minded.

—MM

///

June 1, 2016
Preparedness—10, Professionalism—10, Personality—11

You are truly one of the best teachers in this school. More teachers should be like you. You are very professional and take your classes very seriously, but you are also open to suggestions. And your personality is the best part about you. You are unlike all the boring teachers in this school, which in my opinion, is a good thing.

—AM

==

June 1, 2016
Preparedness—9.5, Professionalism—10, Personality—10

As a class, it is very engaging there is not much to complain about. The only thing I would say is listen out for your name more or have the class be a little quieter. [There were forty-three students in this class. Most were seniors.] Also try and not ramble you kind of lose people when you ramble…

—JQ

//

June 1, 2016

Your performance this year as a teacher was outstanding. You are truly a great and unique soul. Thank you for making my first year as enjoyable as it is 10/10, I would recommend…

—CR

===

June 1, 2016
Preparedness—9, Professionalism—8, Personality—9, Overall—9

You usually have the assignments on the board. You grade and respond to emails quickly and efficiently. You have an awesome personality and although I don't get most of your jokes, I would label them as funny. Although not directly, I see you help students (talk to them when they seem down).

—BS

As previously mentioned, there were a great many graduating seniors in this period, who had been gone for at least a week by this time…and now on to period 7.

//

June 1, 2016
Preparedness—10, Professionalism—9, Personality—10, 10, 10, 10, 10!!!

You are a very prepared man. You start right away as soon as the bell rings and present your things with very approachable.
I give you a 9, only because I think professional people are strict and boring and you are the opposite.

You are the coolest person I know!

—SA

===

June 1, 2016

Your performance this year has been incredible. You're basically the only teacher I wish to have next year. Your ways of innovating the writing technique are untouched and I look at it with a great emotion of joy. During my tenture, [I believe the student means 'tenure.'] in this class, my writing has greatly improved. I also found some joy in writing through this class. Your personal stories only add the new creative things I can add my paragraphs. The depressing, the happy, the monotone writing I have turned in through this school year have greatly impacted my mental viewpoint on some things & changed my perspective on some things forever. Your performance will go down in History, Mr. Fishkind.

—RA

//

June 1, 2016
Preparation—9.5, Professionalism—10, Personality—10

Not going to lie, for some assignments I was kinda lost but I don't entirely say it's your/my fault. Somedays I was not paying attention, some days the way you explained it lost me entirely. But it was all solved by a simple "I don't get it…"

I truly enjoyed the nature of all the assignments and how we connected them to real world events. It allowed me to see them in new lights and explore just how much creativity I have in store.

Every single 'telenovela' moment in my life you were there to advise me, give me a different perspective, and more.

I truly appreciate all that you've done for me. I will miss you until I have you again.

10 out of 10—would take this course again!

—JB

==

June 1, 2016
Preparedness—9, Professionalism—9, Personality—definitely a 10

You are a very good teacher. You seem to be a good elective teacher and a good English teacher. We both know those are two different environments. One con I must add is for you not to take things so personal, such as students leaving your class for personal reasons. This is an enjoyable class. People's tardy or absence has the least to do with you. PS—keep being the best!

—ED

///

June 1, 2016

Love everything especially the more challenging work when it comes to storytelling, like the backwards story.
There's nothing I dislike.

—JD

==

June 1, 2016

Preparedness: I think you did well in being prepared every day with a new writing assignment.
Professionalism: you were pretty professional throughout the year.
Personality: you have a good personality, that enhances the mood of the classroom. I rate you a 9 on a scale of 1–10.

Course survey—I like that in this class I get a chance to pursue a hobby that I hope one day will become my career. I like the degree of freedom in writing stories. The class has been a very good experience for me, so thanks.

—JF

//

June 1, 2016

I love my Creative writing class! I have no complaints. If I could take this class all four years of High School. This is not only my favorite class Mr. Fishkind is my sister and I favorite teacher of all time and forever will be. I always recommend my friends to take this class.

This class isn't just great because it's Creative Writing, but the teacher is actually kind and understanding toward his students.

—EG

===

June 1, 2016

Entering this school year, I was excited to see what the "Fishkind Experience" would be like. I wasn't at all disappointed. First, I was excited b/c I was ending the day with a chill teacher and a person who evoked thought within his class to kids who are in an uninspiring environment. The topics were always fruitful. The professionalism was always on point. The personality was always vibrant & positive. If you ever get discouraged by your colleagues or higher-ups never forget the impact you've left on the lives you've touched!

—KH

//

June 1, 2016

You are always respectful and patient towards all the students even though some of them do not really return it. The schedule is always prepared and well thought-out with reasonable deadlines. Your character is very funny, kind and patient. Don't ever change.

—KH (Not the same one)

==

June 1, 2016

The best part of this class is having the freedom to write about whatever we want to. It is a big relief to have a choice. We can write about whatever comes to mind. I think that since we can create and write whatever we want, we put more effort into it, and we enjoy it.

I can't really say that there are any parts of this class that I don't actually like. Everything is really great and goes really well.

Believe me when I say that you are one of the best teachers I have ever had. I don't have anything negative to say about you or your class. On a scale of 1 to 10, I would rate you a solid 10. I would have no problem taking this class all four years of High School. It is a really great class that we can learn a lot from. I think it's great. Keep all of this the same, don't change.

—JL

//

June 1, 2016

Honestly, this while year was great having you as a teacher. I've never felt right writing somewhere, or safe with writing my honest opinions on things, or expressing my personal feelings. Nor is there a lot of teachers who really care about their students, they all pretend to, but everyone knows our teachers don't worry about us. There's only a handful of teachers that really do care about their students as much as getting paid to teach them. Never have we had to wait on you, or not have an assignment ready for us—preparedness: 10/10 Yes there is very minimal limit in what we write, but when presenting, or turning things in and such, most all be on time and appropriate with the way your class is set up.

Professionalism: 10/10—I've only come across two (2) teachers with such a kind heart, and so much perspective, and selflessness. You're happy, positive and wise personality, has taught me a lot about life and myself. Personality: 100/10—I can go to you for anything, not only as a teacher, but as someone there for me.

—CS

==

June 1, 2016

Preparedness: On a scale of 1–10 I give it a 10. You are always prepared for class and what you have planned for us to do.

Personality: On a scale of 1–10, I give it 1,000,000,000. Most teachers don't have a personality, they are just boring with no sense of humor. This is the opposite with you. I find your class very entertaining with interesting topics to write about. I wouldn't change it in any way. If anyone doesn't enjoy your class, then it means they don't like writing or they are extremely stupid.

—KT

Well, that does it for the end of year evals, now on to the senior letters. You will need tissues…

//

January 16, 2016

My most inspirational person is my Creative writing teacher, Mr. Fishkind, He is one of the best and most down-to-earth people that I have ever met in my entire life. I would also consider him as my best friend. Not only did he care for my well-being as a student, but also as a person. He has helped me with so many things, I honestly would not be here if it weren't for him. He believed in me when I didn't believe in myself. He has made me more confident about my work, and really boosted my self-esteem. Freshman year was the hardest for me, and when he became my English teacher, things started to look up for me. I am now a graduating Everglades High School of the class of 2016! Thank you so much Mr. Fishkind for being an awesome teacher and a great friend.

—XW

===

May 15, 2016

Dear Mr. Fishkind,

Throughout the year you challenged our creative minds into writing various pieces and occasionally had us write letters to various prominent historical figures. You taught us to honor what deserved honor and respect, so today, I write this letter to you, honoring and thanking you for all that you do. You are a great and wonderful teacher and an even bigger source of inspiration. Every day in your class was a discovery and creativity. You taught us that words are a powerful thing, and that art lies not just within the realms of painters and sculptors and musicians but also within the realm of a writer. What is achievable with pen and paper is infinite and I thank you for showing me that. You gave us the opportunity to express ourselves and have a voice and that has no price tag. You took the time to read our work from beginning to end and applauded the talent and potential you saw in each and every one of us. This letter is just a small token of my appreciation; you deserve a novel for such hard work and endless dedication. As I head off to college just know that you will not fade form my memory, you are far too much of an inspiration for me to forget about you. You taught me more than books ever did. I never believed in my work, but you always did. I will take the lessons you've taught me with me on this journey called life and harness my creativity as I go. Thank you times a million!

Sincerely,
DD

///

May 15, 2016

Mr. Fishkind,

These past four years have been tumultuous ones. From the stresses of college entrance exams, to maintaining grades, you are only here to experience one year of my stress, the most stressful one in high school. I arguably have more to go through, 11th. Throughout that time, you've been nothing but a role model to me. You're so full of wisdom in your off-hand sayings and perception of life. I think I've learned more actual life lessons in your class than any class I've taken at EHS. It sucks that you didn't teach Creative writing earlier, I probably would've been set for life! On top of that, all the writing we've done in your class has only pushed me to realize that I had writing abilities I wasn't even aware that I had. Lastly, your continual perseverance whether it be your teaching to the regular level English, or your personal battle with cancer only inspires me to do more. Thank you, I'll be sure to invite you to the White House!

—JP

PS: This is the student who came back to EHS as a faculty member.

==

May 15, 2016

Dear Mr. Fishkind,

    I remember the first day I heard your name. My classmate was talking beside me, sentences an endless stream of mundane babble that often dominated conversations hosted by my peers. I remember thinking, rather incredulously, "what kind of a name is Fishkind?"

    I soon came to learn that Fishkind was the sort of name that belonged to a perfectly eccentric, driven educator, with a natural love of reading, writing and the arts. It was the sort of name that belonged to a teacher that selflessly fostered his student's individuality, their sense of creativity, and the mindfulness that is so often lost in the rigor of the modern-day school system.

    Yet, I was never your student. Our meeting was as happenstance as they came, coming from the sheer coincidence that you were the Young writers Club sponsor.

    You were the first adult in my 12 years of schooling that I truly felt connected to. That are not many older figures in my life that I particularly look up to. In my Senior year, I have begun to see more of these adult figures in my life, predominantly teachers, but you were the first.

    I remember thinking how cool it was to have a teacher so embroiled in the concepts of free expression. I remember you strumming your guitar, my eyes closed and mind open as I allowed myself to go from the daily stresses harsh curriculums and an increasingly complicated life at home, if only for a little bit.

    It is increasingly apparent how much you care about your kids. Time after time, you proved this even at the expense of your own finances. Even when our clubs rarely (if ever) broke even, you still continued to encourage us to stage such events, particularly if they would give us a chance in the spotlight. Some of my best high school memories were spent in your classroom among the Young Writers Club.

The whirlwind of college prep and AP work has caught up with me this year and I often found myself regretting that I have not taken the time to visit or say hello to you more often. Even if business has made me a stranger, I sincerely hope you can understand how much I appreciate your actions, bit as an educator and as a role model.

Thank you for being there for me first.

Sincerely,
EG

//

May 15, 2016

Thank you, Mr. Fishkind, for a chance at graduation. This is something that I will forever be grateful for. I'm not a person of much words, but this good deed you did for me really means a lot.

Sincerely,
AD

==

May 15, 2016

Dear Mr. Fishkind,

This is, as we both know, the second and last time I'll have you as my teacher. I still remember you from Freshman year—you were a calmer change from Mrs. V. And I also thought your mustache was cool. [The amount of times I bragged about it to my friends, I couldn't even count on a finger.] You always taught me a lot, about music, about writing, about literature. Your class was always one I enjoyed, and to this day, I still do.

I was excited to hear you got the Creative Writing class, and since, I've tried to get a spot. It finally happened. I have immensely enjoyed being challenged. Your ability to make me think and have fun at the same time still impresses me. Only a handful of teachers in my lifetime have been able to accomplish such a feat. We've written on so many topics, now too! I have been diversified as a writer, and now I know I have improved. I am sure that I will never forget anything that we went through, from Francesca to sonnets and more.

Thank you for being such a good educator to me. Thank you for exposing to things that I wouldn't have otherwise. Thank you for being kind and compassionate to everyone. THANK YOU for being YOU! Never forget me, okay?

Yours truly,
AB

///

May 15, 2016

Dear Mr. Fishkind,

I am writing you just out of sheer appreciation of the great teacher you've been in the past. I know you're usually the one who has wanted to write letters for me, but I couldn't help thinking of you when I was asked to write to the teachers who helped me develop into the great student I am now. Because of you years ago, I was able to find amusement in my writing and this encouraged me to keep writing and keep improving it. I no longer roll my eyes at the sight of a new essay or anecdote assignment; I just avidly look forward to the challenge due to myriads of 'warm-ups' you made our class acquiesce to two years ago. I guess the famous saying: 'you'll thank me later...' it is an actual thing. Again, thank you Mr. Fishkind for being such a great teacher to me in the past. I hope you inspire many more plethora of students and that we keep in contact so that one day you can finally write me that 'recommendation letter' you keep bragging about, ha-ha.

Sincerely,
JC

==

May 15, 2016

Dear Mr. Fishkind,

I am writing this in my AP Literature class to thank you for helping me as a student, a person and a writer. One of the letters I wrote was meant to be a surprise, and this does not count because I am sure you already know how much I appreciate all your help. You encouraged me to pursue my passion as a writer, and it was on your suggestion that I originally looked into UCF, which I will now be attending. Our class gave me time and tools to write, and some of my best work got done in the free time that you gave me. I hope that I can be as good of a writer as you believe I will be.

Thank you for being my teacher,

Sincerely,

JT

(This student has become a journalist for the *Sun-Sentinel*.)

///

May 15, 2016

Dear Mr. Fishkind,

You're probably not expecting to hear from me, but you were a bigger help to me than you think. Your English class was the first English class I was successful in. you were always encouraging me and being positive. You helped me realize I was smart and that I can succeed if I put my effort into it.

Also, I feel I was one of the only ones who appreciated your many jokes. You helped me gain a confidence in myself to succeed in what I do, and for that, I say a sincere thank you. Here I am, about to graduate, and accepted into FIU, and I can say a big part of it was from your guidance Sophomore year.

Thank you, Mr. Fishkind,

LC

==

May 15, 2016

Dear Mr. Fishkind,

No contest—you will always be my most memorable Freshman year teacher. I can still remember thinking that I was lucky not having any portable classes that year. Then, after the first week, we suddenly shifted into a new portable room. The level of disappointment was immense; my old classroom was only a few feet away from my new destination. However, all that frustration dissipated when I got to meet my new teacher. I have never had so much fun in an English class, except maybe this year. You were always my vote for best hair!

NL

//

May 15, 2016

Dear Mr. Fishkind,

I know I haven't done a good job of turning in your work for class and I am SOOOOOOO sorry, but I thoroughly enjoyed my time in your class even though I spent most of it talking. I admire your dedication and ability to read all of our work every day, grade our work and still be able to interact with your student. You're funny, witty and give really good advice that I will keep in mind as I mature and meet new people. I know it is hard teaching all these underclassmen who don't want to learn and don't appreciate you but just stay strong and try to teach the kinds you can. I am very grateful Steven convinced me to take your class and I will always keep you in memory.

Sincerely,
RF

==

May 15, 2016

Dear Mr. Fishkind,

I am very thankful to you for having always encouraged me to learn more, to practice more and to work hard for what I wanted. I am very thankful for every warm-up (very creative topics by the way) that you made me do; I am so glad for every advice you gave me, for always pushing me to practice my English, to learn more vocabulary and for all those essays that you assigned. I'm thankful for the concerts where you liked to play the guitar and sing (in Spanish a few times, which was actually horrible, but you definitely tried for all of us). I'm so grateful to have had the opportunity of being in your class, you are a great teacher, the funny, kind, very social and a little crazy too. Thank you for being patient with me when I tried to communicate in my broken English. Thank you, because I know that no matter what, I can always count on you.

Sincerely,
AF

///

May 15, 2016

To Mr. Fishkind,

I really enjoyed your class last year. I figured out that I could have fun with writing and that it's not all essays and structure. I want to thank you for that. Now I can write other things more freely, because I believe that the best things have a little twist to them. I'm not great at writing letters but thank you for the creative assignments and your great class. It was easily my favorite class last year.

From,
MM

May 13, 2016

Dear Mr. Fishkind,

You believed in me since day one when I was transferred to your first period English class in Freshman year (it was English I honors) we began our four-year journey in Everglades at the same time and we've gotten so far. I'm more than grateful for having you as a teacher for 3 years. You helped enrich my creative side and never failed to give me a daily challenge to think through.

You were always great for advice but the time I needed it most was actually this year when I couldn't seem to get my life together to decide where it is, I wanted to go. To you, it may not have seemed like much what you said to me was much, but it was one piece of advice more that helped me rethink the way I was trying to decide. Your advice helped me out of that bubble where FIU is commonly thought of as a lower tier school. It took listening to your input, visiting the campus, doing my research and of course, doing their financial aid that helped me realize that this was the school that was going to give mem everything I want in college.

Mr. Fishkind, I thank you so much for everything. For being a cool teacher, for believing in me every step of the way, helping me with letters of recommendation and giving me knowledge that will help me in the real world. Thank you so much.

Sincerely yours,

NC

PS—those who dream by day are cognizant of many things that escape those who dream at night EAP.

//

May 15, 2016

Mr. Fishkind,

There's nothing I have ever been more anxious to turn in, complete, or give to any of my teachers more than this appreciate letter I am writing to you. Though I write one for all my teachers, I can honestly say that this one is most sincere. This is not just another 'appreciation letter', I can assure you. This is a document expressing the true gratefulness I feel to you as a student and friend. With summer approaching, it is only appropriate I give you this now (though I've been waiting a long time to do so)

First, and most importantly, I want to address your remarkable teaching methods. Not only have you been an exceptional instructor as far as intelligence and being prepared, but you also have shown an enormous amount of support towards myself and all your students. You brush off all the negative occurrences between yourself and certain students and teach them on a completely new slate each day. Though much of my gratitude was expressed yesterday (when we wrote on what you should improve on as a teacher) this is the proper document that you should receive and deserve. You are a friend to me and all the students and support us unconditionally in our academic journey. The work you give is actually useful both in school and in the real world!

One object you are most memorable for is your interesting, and if may say so myself, groovy taste in music. Your music warmups are something I'm really going to miss! On a personal level, you have shown me the amazing character I have within myself. and have boosted my self-confidence and reassured me of my ability to achieve and accomplish. Some things I'm going to remember are the day you used keratin on your hair, and everyone freaked out, the awesome days you wore jeans to school, the day you played your great music for us on your guitar, and of course, the day you dressed as a wizard (radical costume, I must say) [It was Halloween].

We both know there aren't enough words to express how someone feels. There aren't enough adjectives to describe just how inspirational or beautiful something is. However, if you never stop teaching, and provide hundreds of more students the opportunity to experience such a talented teacher, musician, advisor and friend. Thank you for all the overtime you do for us, the drive to and from school each day, the unpaid hours you stay to complete work, the time you take to grade papers, the hours you've spent planning lessons, and everything else you do. Thank you, a million times, and more for the wonderful year you have gifted me and the rest of your students with.

Sincerely,
COC

PS: This student has gone on to become a pilot!

///

And now, we move on to a new year—2016–2017. This was a transitional year as creative writing was given to another teacher, and what did I get? One class of English 3 regulars (a group of chronic underachieving juniors with attitudes to match) and five intensive reading classes. My wife urged me to quit rather than accept this. I deferred, saying I would try it out for a year (of course, I had to work on the Reading Endorsement—five courses of continuing ed joy, not) So needless to say, this was a change in what was going on. Also, the school changed schedule from seven fifty-minute periods to A/B ninety-minute period block scheduling, which meant I would only see my students every other day. This also changed the dynamic (albeit slightly) of my relationships with my students, but you can be the judge as to how much this affected how they and I worked together. Read and enjoy!

===

Period 3
Intensive Reading

June 1, 2017

This year has been quite interesting. My experience with this year jumped around from just anger and stress. Although I've had good a good year with most of my teachers. Sure, some teachers were questionable, but I pulled through.

Your performance was a 10/10. Although I would recommend a little less work just like 1 page. Also, your music interests are very interesting. Still, you're a great teacher and would recommend students to hear your lectures.

—JC

///

June 1, 2017

This school year went on quite fast. There are definitely some bad days but most of it were okay. I have decent grades since first to last quarter. All my HomeWorks, projects, class works and quizzes, I did them all. My teachers were nice and helped me so much this year. All my hard work payed off. I am proud of myself and so does my family.

Mr. Fishkind, your way of teaching is very unique. Despite all of the work you've gave us every single day, I still enjoyed it and understand English better. I admire how you share your personal experiences with us, and how inspiring it is to me. I also wish to have the ability to talk like you, using big, advanced vocabulary words in every sentence you say.

Thank you, Mr. Fishkind, for everything. And as much as I enjoyed your class, I wish I'll be able to get out of it. And I'm positive that I will. Thank you.

—DD

===

June 1, 2017

In the beginning of the year, I was very upset and angry. I was very disappointed to land myself in a Reading class because I haven't had one since the 7th grade. But I told myself that I was put here for a reason. So, I just sucked it up and went with it.

Your personality is 10/10 but your music can be questionable sometimes. You were definitely one of my teachers that I did not despise this year. I think you did a fabulous job this school year.

Although I'm really excited to leave this class, I'm going to miss you. Thank you for everything.

—AL

//

June 1, 2017

This year to me education-wise was pretty good. The only class I actually had trouble with was Geometry. I met a lot of cool people. I also worked a lot harder this year than last year. This year to me was a success. Mr. Fishkind to me is 10/10. He helped us improve in Reading a lot. Although he is sometimes sarcastic and a little rude, I enjoyed having him as a teacher. I am glad he witnessed me grow over the year.

—GM

==

June 1, 2017

Overall, this school year wasn't what I expected it to be. My grades were good, but I still need to do better in Math. In this class alone I have learned many things I didn't know before. For example, one thing we learned that I found interesting was how to tell if someone is lying. I really enjoyed that, and I look forward to next year.

If I had to rate your teaching, professionalism and preparedness on a scale from 1 to 10 it would be a 10. This is because every day you had new work for us. Also, I don't think you ever missed a day this year which shows professionalism. I really enjoyed this class and learned something new every day.

—AR

///

June 1, 2017

Stressful: schoolwork and homework had me tied up. At first, I was ready for school to be over with but, I joined the soccer team and we finished in 2nd place. This year I've done more than I imagined. After all the goods and bads, I'm thankful for life and I'm happy.

To be honest Mr. Fishkind, you are one of the best teachers I've had this year. On my top 2 list. You are always prepared to teach class; you handle obstacles well. Your performance is great because you make eye contact, attract and keep attention when you read.

—SS

==

June 1, 2017

To me the whole school experience I had this year was alright, except for the fact that it was so tiring to me, it wasn't all that hard to keep up with all my classes but since I'm almost most of the time tired I always feel pretty lazy in class or at home. So, my GPA dropped a little since I started this school year. One thing that I did not enjoy this year was my French class, that class was the main reason my GPA dropped this school year.

—LT

She was so tired she did not follow the prompt for the day… oh well.

//

June 1, 2017

Where do I begin? How do I start this? I can't say that I have many things to say that had changed me as a person. Compared to myself when I entered 10th grade, I would say I had changed my view about things. I'm glad that I was able to draw and was able to express my interest about "things." At the end I'm just a hypocrite saying that I didn't change. Someone when cling on regrets. Someone who want to change but scared to. Someone who make a big deal about everything. That is me, and I won't ever change that.

Our (or my) 10th grade Reading teacher, Mr. Fishkind, he the type who make students do work during breaks. He is the type to give us work every day. He doesn't teach us, but he gives us work to harness our "skill.' Mr. Fishkind make his student work til no end. I'm the one to judge because I never do his work. I do believe that I can improve if I did the work but I blame only myself for laziness. I can only wish that he'll teach us, so we know what to do rather than copying from other people.

—KT

Yes, it's true that copying is not learning…now on to period 4—Intensive Reading.

===

May 30, 2017

My overall year was great. I achieved many goals. My goals were to get good grades, done. To get out of my comfort zone and overcome my shyness, done.

And just be an all-around better person, done. I told myself I could do it and I did, and I wish to next year.

Mr. Fishkind you were always prepared, you had what we needed on the board at all times. You never slacked at being a teacher you were always ready (to deal with this very annoying 4th period). Overall, I had a great year and I'm going to take a few tips from you and use them in life. You were always professional nothing really more than that.

—NA

///

May 30, 2017

My Sophomore year in High School was good and it flew by. This was my fastest year of school.

Not only that, but I also met my best friend. All my teachers was good except my Spanish, she always gave me trouble. But my Reading teacher always wants the best for me. I had trouble with my grades a little but overall, my year was good.

My Reading teacher Mr. Fishkind was a great teacher. He was very professional, he never cursed, nor did he get mad. If anything annoyed him, he gave chances then he would move you, then eventually kick you out. But he rarely kicked anyone out. He was very prepared. Every day I would walk in and he was ready to work and teach. His performance was great I rate him 10/10. We had our rough patch in the first semester, but I asked if I could restart, and he said yeah. Ever since then we have been good.

—MB

==

May 30, 2017

This year has pretty interesting for me. It was a year of transition because I moved from another state to here, I had to adapt to the new school and the people. I learned a lot, not only academically but personally. Made new friends and had no problem with school or other people. My grades are good, but they could be better. Overall, I had a good year in which I had fun learning and experiencing new things.

I think that you did a great job teaching us and preparing us for the FSA. We learned a lot and even though it was a lot of work it helps us improve ourselves academically. Also, you gave us a lot of good life tips and taught us that you have to work and give your best for the things you want in life. To be honest you are one of the most professional, organized and prepare teacher that I've ever had because the system that you use in your classroom it's really good. You're a great teacher and I'll miss your class. Overall, I give you a 10.

—LC

///

May 30, 2017

This year for me has been interesting to say the least. There are classes I hated and classes I never had a problem with. For 2nd period 2-D studio Art, it was never hard or complicated. And there are moments in Mr. Cox's that I actually find interesting. For 2nd period PE it is what it is. I never hated it, I actually loved it. For 3rd period English, it was just as good as 2-D Studio Art. For 4th period Intensive Reading it was annoying for the reason I was in the class but understandable. Either way I never hated it either.

For 5th period Spanish, it was the same as PE, but I didn't love it as much. As for 6th period Geometry, I started hating Geometry and

I still hate Geometry. For Biology, probably the best class ever, higher than 2-D Art. And finally, for 8th period, it's study hall.

I would rate Mr. Fishkind's performance at maximum proficiency. In professionalism, there are times when he explains something as easy as it is. In preparedness, Mr. Fishkind prepared me for the midterm and the unit tests. He especially was helpful at facilitating the units to easily understand it.

—DC

===

May 30, 2017

This year has been very stressful, annoying and filled with anxiety, but overall, it was unforgettable. I met people that have changed my life and I have changed myself for the better. I had a lot of fun as a sophomore, but I can't wait to become a Junior.

Mr. Fishkind was a great teacher to have. I believe he has taught me many new strategies about reading better and comprehending what I have read, and with his help, I believe I passed the FSA reading test.

—ND

///

May 30, 2017

This year has been good for me because I had set goals coming into my Sophomore year. Those goals were getting good grades, basketball and graduating. One goal is on pause for right now. But I won't give up. So far, I ended up with all A's and B's. So, this is one reason why this year has been good. Another reason is basketball. I didn't wat to play for the school, but I wanted to play travel ball. It's very hard to get into this travel basketball team cause they are great. They picked me up to be on the team and there's a chance I could get offers. So, this is the other reason why this year has been great for me.

Rate: I rate myself [another one who missed what the prompt said...oy...] as a 10 in professionalism, a 9 on preparedness and a 9 on performance.

—DD

==

May 30, 2017

All in all, my Sophomore year was pretty appalling. Academically my expectations were far too high than what I actually do. I signed up for AP World and little did I know that was the worst decision of my life. The countless nights staying up and doing homework for the rest of my classes because I spent the day doing my normal homework.

Although the school year wasn't the best, this class was pretty okay. Although it was a little overboard with the work, I fell as though I needed it to pass the FSA. However, after the FSA, I don't feel we needed to work as much as we did. All in all, I rater this class and Mr. Fishkind an 8.

—MH

///

May 30, 2017

This year has been a setback for me as I have to pick up on my work and advance [?] in my schoolwork. Mr. Fishkind's performance was better than expected.

His professionalism was better than most teachers and actually cared about your grade. He has prepared me for the FSA [teaching to the test—yes, I know...] and I hope I pass it with flying colors.

—M

==

May 30, 2017

    This year for me has been medium for me. It wasn't too hard or too easy. As for the workload was a lot but once you got used to it's not that hard. Mr. Fishkind is very generous and gives you a lot of time to finish your work. He gives you plenty of time to do your work. If I were to rate my performance, I would say it's okay. I probably could have finished my assignments faster. And there were times where I didn't do my projects on time. And sometimes I didn't have all my materials, such as paper.

—AO

//

May 30, 2017

    This school year has been stressful and boring. I feel like I've worked harder this school year than any other which is good. I tried my best to maintain good grades, but French/Geometry was always an issue. Which made it hard to get A/B report card maybe even all As.

    Your performance, Mr. Fishkind excellent as always. You never fail to make sure a student succeeds his/her goals. You are a very hard-working teacher and a fast grader.

—WP

==

May 30, 2017

    My Sophomore year of High School has been very educational and experimental [!]. I went form a school I knew everyone, and I was one of the 'popular' kids to going to a brand-new school where I knew nobody, changing schools was hard but now it's getting easier.

Mr. Fishkind in my opinion is an amazing teacher. Even though his students don't pay attention or care that he trys his best to teach us. His performance is always the best always has a schedule (schedule) on the board to know what youre doing every time we get to class.

—AV

//

Period 5
Intensive Reading

May 31, 2017

This year has been alright, did the best in academics in years [!] and your performance as a teacher was amazing, one of the few teachers I wish I could have again.

—JA

===

May 31, 2017

This year has been very challenging. But I made it through thankfully. My teachers this year are very hard-working and made sure we are passing and doing well. I've been studying and making sure I don't fall out of focus. I've placed at my Debate competitions. All in all, this year was really enjoyable.

However, Mr. Fishkind's performance has been quite well. His teaching skills helps us learn more every day. He sure does give a lot of work, but it helps. He has also pushed me to read more. He is also of course prepared. There has never been a day in this class where you don't do anything. Mr. Fishkind is professional too, he has never raised his voice. I would rate Mr. Fishkind as a great teacher.

—AB

//

May 31, 2017

This year for me was an emotional roller-coaster. It could have gone better, but it didn't. Teachers and students were annoying along with my personal problems at home. I would probably rate this year a 7 out of 10. I didn't get the grades I wanted except for the last quarter. Some moments were good like when I started going out with my girlfriend, Niyah. Other moments were bad, like when I almost got into a fight.

Mr. Fishkind has been a good teacher, I guess. He has some moments where he's annoying, but you can tell he really cares a lot about his students. I think he can do better with listening and not talking over people. I don't think he should give people as much work as he does. It is very overwhelming especially if you are already behind. I also believe he shouldn't work us every day all year. Even the best teachers don't push 100% every single day.

—CD

===

May 31, 2017

My 2017 school year was quite a bit bumpy at the beginning of the year. As soon as I let my mistakes get past me it started to become a better year. Towards the end of the year my life got better by having astonishing grades for myself getting my life together by having a job and a couple of responsibilities.

Mr. Fishkind will receive a 10/10 rate from me. Even when there was situations where he could've lost his mind, he stayed cool calm and collective. Overall, his professionalism and performance was outstanding, one of the best, if not the best teacher in Everglades High school.

—KG

//

May 31, 2017

This year during this class a learned a lot. It was a great experience. It was sort of a fun class sometimes but most of the time it was a lot of work. But overall, it was not a bad class I have had worse classes.

My teacher was a great teacher. He really explained a lot and gave me many useable tips for the future. He was very professional for the whole year. He was the most prepared teacher I ever had. Always had a lesson plan and goal.

Whenever someone needed a pen or paper, he had it for them. His overall performance was a 10/10. Great work!!!

—BG

===

May 31, 2017

Sophomore year was mostly the same as freshman year but it mostly harder in a way depending on the teachers you have. Some teachers were more respectful than others but some also exaggerate on the assignments that are due in a certain day. In Sophomore year you know more the people you meet last year, and you could get new friends or enemies.

The most common thing in Sophomore year is that everyone likes to cheat [!] one way or another. And also, more candy sellers have popped up around the school to buy candy which makes a lot of money because of the scarce of sugar trans food.

Mr. Fishkind is one of some honest people I have met throughout the year. His performance in daily work is excessive but acceptable with the amount of time we get to complete it. He is respectful with us and understands how we feel discoust [disgust?] with the other teachers in the school. One annoying thing is that his music is too loud to hear your own music, which some of us don't even know what type it is. [They did not get progressive rock—*lol.*] And last but not least, he knows all of us in one way or another.

—DH

///

May 31, 2017

This year has been a good experience overall. I've learned way more than what I learned last year. My vocabulary has improved. Not only have it improved but I learned how to use them in sentences and in my daily vocabulary, but I learned how to cite textual evidence better. Before I came to this class, I didn't know anything about citing textual evidence I've improved so much compared to last year.

Your performance this year was good. If we didn't understand anything you made sure that we understood things better. You were always prepared to teach, and you expected us to be prepared to learn. When you spoke, you gave direct eye contact to each student. There was never a day when were confused.

—BM

==

May 31, 2017

This school year was okay because I had trouble in Spanish 1 it was hard. You know how speak it. The other classes I pass. I mean I work so hard because I am trying to go to college. The only thing I hate about school is test.

Mr. Fishkind is a good teacher. He loves what he is doing but I think he assigns too much work. And that it.

—QM

//

May 31, 2017

This year has been great. In this class I feel like I actually learned a lot. Literature wise and socially wise. The work was a lot of numbers, but fairly easy. It's been a good one with my boy Fishkind.

Mr. Fishkind has been incredible this year. I've never entered this classroom without doing a lot of work. I've never this classroom and seen a substitute. His attendance is perfection, and his teaching skills are out of this world. Hopefully I can have him again next year for English 3.

—CM

==

May 31, 2017

My school year this year has been alright. Towards second quarter I started to slack off. Because the grade was short, and things were happening at that time as well out of school. Towards third quarter I started to actually try with big test started to study busting in the effort.

On rating Mr. Fishkind 1–10 I would give him a 9.5 only because there would be a moment where he would want like 50 pages of work, and it would be such little time to complete it. Besides the fact of that, he okay. Very lay back and chill, never pressure anybody about anything, gives you the chance to make up your work, gives you many chances and I couldn't be upset about that.

—RM

//

May 31, 2017

   This year was really hard for me. I was not expecting this year
to be so frustrating. I was hoping that this school year would be the
same as my old school back in Puerto Rico. It was extremely hard
for me at the beginning of the year because I came to a country with
hardly any friends in Miami, and different ways of communicating.
I knew I couldn't be myself because I didn't want any conflict with
other people. But the thing that hurt me the most moving here was
that I had to start from scratch.

   But this year wasn't just me complaining about my life's change
pout of all the bad that had happened to me there some things that
I'm happen. I met a lot of new friends in this school who expect
[accept?] me for who I am, a really funny, emotional and annoying.
I met other people form outside school. My past friendships from
Puerto Rico have grown even more and better. And most importantly if it wasn't for me coming to the states, I wouldn't have met the
most beautiful girl I've ever met in the worldwide world.

   Mr. Fishkind your performance during this year has been very
challenging from you giving us a lot of work. To me where sometimes
never sleeping. To me barely doing good work. In your class. But I've
noticed you're so far have been the toughest English teacher I've ever
met in my life. But also, the best because I've learned a lot this school
year and if it wasn't for you, I wouldn't have probably done well, in
the FSA test. And also helped me with your drive and motivating and
pushing us to be the best we can in this world.

                                                              —DMM

==

May 31, 2017

   This school year has been great for me. I feel as though I have
improved and finally learned what it means to be a student-ath-

lete. Although I have done well in my classes I still dislike how my Geometry teacher taught and instructed our classes. [They gave the name, but I will not share it.]

You are a very hard-working teacher with a great outlook on life and your job. Keep working and less work towards the end of the year!!!!!!

—RR

///

May 31, 2017

This year has been better for me than last year. But I know I could have done better. Next year I'll start working harder put work in on time & miss less work. I'll study harder & get better grades.

For your performance, I'd say it's very good. Your teaching is understandable & stable. Your preparedness is on point & your performance is good. Only problem is how much work is supposed to be done in a short amount of time. But there's always time to improve.

—MR

==

May 31, 2017

Your performance as a teacher was great in my opinion. You always seemed to have though your assignments ahead to help explain to your students better.

When some students would act up you never raised your voice like other teachers you always kept calm. My rate is 8/10.

—FS

//

May 31, 2017

This year has been very difficult for me. I feel like I have grown as a person. By this I mean coming out of my shell more often and stepping out of my comfort zone. Although this is great, I feel like I have not improved academically. This year has been a ling year of self-growth. I feel though like I have lost some motivation for school and doing well in it. I feel like I am slowly gaining more motive to do better in school.

Mr. Fishkind has helped me in some shape or form by pushing me to read more often. He has showed me that reading, and knowledge is power. Although id not always enjoy his class, like for example when presenting, I feel as it is worth it. Not only have I been taught academically, but also been taught life lessons.

—AS

==

May 31, 2017

This year has been very tough for me. I made some bad friends, dated the wrong people, and made some of the worst decisions of my life. I would re-do this whole year if I could. However, I can't do that, so I look at this year as a learning experience. This year is basically a guideline on what not to do for the next two years of High School.

You have been a great teacher. You always explained whatever we were learning very thoroughly and with humor. You remained very professional by not screaming at the kids that got on your nerves and never cursing. You always made the lessons interesting and fun. You give a lot of work but nothing we can't handle. You did great this year Fishkind.

—ST

//

May 31, 2017

This school year has been very stressful for me. Teachers worrying about tests instead of teaching the lesson so we could understand and ace the test. My History teacher was the best, she didn't give too much unnecessary work and she taught her subject (instead of just handing out work to us). Mr. Fishkind is a good teacher. He loves what he's doing. But I think he assigns too much work. And that's about it.

—JT

===

May 31, 2017

This year was the worst school year for me in High School. Geometry was not working out well for me, and all my other classes been on and off this year. Geometry was horrible because of miscommunication with the instructor, and the lack of motivation in the instructor teaching.

Fishkind has been the most inspirational teacher I've ever had. Each lesson he gives us something to think about. Which relates what happens in the real world and he is always tying it in to the lesson.

10/10 for everything.

—GV

//

May 31, 2017

This year has been great b/c it open my eyes to get ready for Junior year. I've also found out who are my true friends. Not only did I make it through my Geometry class, but also my Debate class too. I'm glad to say next year hopefully it would be just as great as this year (education wise) Mr. Fishkind has help tremendously w/ my reading. I've learn skills that I hope to take and use all the way to college. His performance and professionalism are awesome. He has showed and gave us more insight to the stories and poems we have read. I'm glad that we did a comprehensive strategies b/c it helps the reader understand what they're reading better. Hope you have a good summer and great class like us next year.

—SW

===

Period 6
English 3 Regular

May 31, 2017

If I were to describe this school year, I would describe it as a productive and eventful school year. I've had the privilege to try new extra-curricular programs and classes. I've had a goal this year and that was to achieve greatness and step closer to my all-time goal of entering into the medical field after graduation.

Mr. Fishkind is a wise teacher, who I can say had properly prepared me for the FSA. In the little time I was in his class, I really wish I was there from the start. His assignments and work were easily doable and can be accomplished within the given time. I very much appreciate his time frame of two days with the 'ticket out the door' system, it allows me to do my work accordingly and not procrastinate. I can honestly say Mr. Fishkind is an extraordinary teacher. Since my very first day in his class, he gave off a great impression as a teacher and still does.

—YA

==

May 31, 2017

In this year was so good and can share with more people.
In December to January, I did a change of school from Franklin
Academy and I came back again because I don't like that school. But
I know more people and to somebody very specially.

This year, I had problems with something class but already
solved the problems and I'm good now. I have good grades and
always learn more English or try to do.

I think that you are a good teacher and helps that need be help.
Maybe you send much work but it's your job.

—LC

///

May 31, 2017

So far, this year has been full of unexpected events. I've shown
hard work in my classes and my grades there has been some errors/
delays that occurred in my classes like leftover work/missing assignments, luckily, I've been focused on those equally as my schoolwork. Finding my classes have been a challenge at first, but now I
had the opportunity (give me 2 weeks). I can find my classes easily
enough without my schedule. My classes are settling for me and I've
grown very attached to them like: Biology, study Hall, Gym, Art
and Intensive Reading. Biology is one of my favorites because I love
science and, in the class, I've been rewarded with intensive rarely
improved grades (A to B+).

The experiments have always surprise me, some students find
the experiments disgusting but I find them cool and interesting. I can
never hate Study Hall because I can finish my leftover assignments
and I can use the computer to go on pinnacle, vocabulary.com, or
usually unblocked games. Gym has been my favorite through and
through because I love running and playing sports. Art is one of the

easiest classes I have, I can draw pictures and explain the warmups/questions based on the work. Intensive Reading is without a doubt my favorite because it is quiet, and I sometimes get to read my books whenever there's no work needed to be finished. I go on pinnacle 2–3 times in a school week, my grades in my classes rarely change. The most is Spanish because of the unchecked work that I don't give her because she doesn't notify her students about it. Of course, if I need help in my work/don't understand the grade I have right now, there's always an option to go to the learning lab. This place has always been my 'training wheels' in other words, it's a place to help students work on their assignments, check pinnacle and help what to do to improve his/her grade. My parents have trusted me to finish my work and check pinnacle to see how I can improve my grade.

—DC

I believe this student missed the prompt entirely…in English class…says a lot about me…oy…

===

May 31, 2017

This school year has been great. I got back together with Jonathan and Adam and I became bff's with Shelby. Me and Jonathan have known each other since Middle School. This year has been crazy. I had a sweet sixteen. I got a new bestie. I got good grades and moving on to my 3rd year of High School.

You are the best English teacher I ever had. You are the most professional teacher with a little bit of funny. You were always very prepared. Your performance as a teacher was amazing. Thank you for getting me ready for the FSA.

—LD

//

May 31, 2017

My experience in this school in this semester that have I have been here was and still is very good and met mane [many] friends and teacher who are very good, each one in its different type of is unforgettable experience in this school there is much to learn. [This student arrived in the third quarter and knew zero English.]

I found this school very good because of all that it offers of learning and in the little that have learned and learned many things.

Fishkind—is a good teacher and learned many things is very good person.

—RE

==

May 31, 2017

This school year has been so good to me. You should be asking yourself: why was it good to you? It was good to me because I've been getting better grades during this year. On the 16th of March I passed the Algebra EOC (during my birthday) and that is something that I wanted to achieve from a long time. During this school year, I grew as a person. I am more responsible now and I have better friends now.

Mr. Fishkind, during this school year you've been teaching me a lot of good stuff and I really appreciate it. You're one of the best teachers in this school and I'm not saying that just because I'm your student, I really mean it.

Your professionalism has been perfect., your performance has been perfect 100 Mr. Fishkind, thank you for being my teacher this year and I hope you have a nice summer.

—RF

//

May 31, 2017

This year has been thoughtful for me. It was thoughtful because I learned a lot during this year. I learned mostly things in school. I learned a lot of things in subjects like: Math and English. I've also learned how to learn.

Mr. Fishkind's performance is great. Mr. Fishkind is a professional person when it comes to teaching. He's serious when he needs to be serious. Mr. Fishkind is always prepared. We are always kept busy with work and we're always doing something. His is really good. He is everything a teacher should be.

—SK

==

May 31, 2017

This year has been a good year for me it was fun and had some good times. It was better than last year I can say that much. The teachers were better and so were my grades. Also, I got a girlfriend for the first time. I had a great time, play video games with my friends and becoming vice president of the comic book club.

If I were to rate how you were this year on preparedness it was great. You really helped me pass the FSA this year. On your performance it was weird in the beginning how you acted but you grew on me and I really enjoyed coming to your class. Your professionalism was good. You really cared about everyone's grades. If I was going to be honest, you are one of the best teachers I've ever met. Thanks for a great year.

—AL

//

May 31, 2017

This year for me has not been very good for me. I have not put forth the necessary effort to do as good as I am capable of doing. If I continue my High School career in this manner I will not graduate. I have recognized that and plan to do better next year.

As a teacher I have to say that you are one of the most dedicated teachers I have ever met. You always do whatever you can to make sure your students understand the matter, whether it be curriculum based or not. You definitely prepared me very well for the FSA as I felt very much capable of the questions, and you did everything possible to make sure your students were prepared. You are definitely the perfect example of what a teacher should be.

—CL

==

May 31, 2017

His year had its ups and downs—got into a few fights, going through a break-up, twice and dealing with family members. Btu other than that things pretty well for the year so far. I been to so many for me parties that I couldn't remember.

To be honest, I was confused with Mr. Fishkind's personality. How he shows his traits to people. But I like it that way. And the way he teach is a way I like every English teacher I have for this school year to be. Everything I learned from him may just help me for next year.

—SM

//

May 31, 2017

That years was very good for me, because I achieved complete the majority of my goals. I achieved improve my grades and achieve improve in football & that year achieve my grades in English, but I have to improve more to reach my goal.

Mister Fishkind is one of the best teachers that I already had in my life. I achieved learn a lot with him. Mister Fishkind is always very responsible and always is in school, never miss one day of class. I have luck for having had that teacher.

—JPM

==

May 31, 2017

This year was a very big change in my life because I left my country to come to the United States. I like it here, but I still have not gotten used to everything, the school was a big difference for me, but when adapted, I really like the person I became, both school and normal. The school taught me a lot and English became my favorite subject. I learned a lot and I learned a little of the language, even if for me it is very difficult.

Mr. Fishkind stands out for his way of teaching, being very charismatic and intelligent at the same time, is my favorite class and teacher. In Brazil, his subject is called 'Literature' I am very happy with what I learned here. I do not know how to thank he for the opportunity to come here and learn new things.

—BM

//

May 31, 2017

This school year was something else because all the work most of the time didn't understand like Geometry, most of the things we got taught we didn't understand at all, but all my other classes I did good. It was Geometry that really messed me up this year, but other than that it was good. I'm still living great, so that's good.

Mr. Fishkind helped me well this year. There is a lot of things I understand about doing because of how he helped use context clues to understand words more clearly. He's helped me know words I never knew before. He's a very good teacher and he's the only teacher I know that hasn't missed a day of school, even when he had cancer. He's a bright man and teaches a lot.

—DO

===

May 31, 2017

This school year has been almost done, I have a lot of experiences and challenge myself tough works and classes. I think Geometry Hon class is a rough class and I am struggle with it. Biology Hon is my favorite subject where I have more opportunities to learn about living things, and science. Photography is the class I don't like, and I didn't focus on this class. English is not my favorite, but I learned how to work harder and focus on my work. However, I think this year has been amazing, interesting that I have more chance to study this class I like, challenge myself with tough class, it also fun year that I have more friends and it really fun to work with them.

Mr. Fishkind is my favorite teacher, before having him as a teacher, my friends told me he is a nice teacher and that is true. Mr. Fishkind really passion to his job, he prepares classwork, very organized that every time you walk past his door, there's always assignments on the board. He is a professional teacher that he always explains everything if we don't understand, and he always make us feel comfortable. He is an easy teacher, but rough when reteaching a lesson. His lesson is very attractive and interesting basically that he is so good a teacher with passion. I will rate him 5 stars because he is an amazing teacher.

—YNP

//

May 31, 2017

From the time I came to Everglades High, my year has been good. I made some new friends, and my grades were on point. The crow here at Everglades are distinct & everyone is their own person and does their own thing. The students have good senses of humor & I talk well with people with good vibes. I was very positive this school year and focused more on my schoolwork than on people, although I attended a couple of parties to get my mind off all the work. The school overall is a good school, but the campus is small and crowded & could be better.

The teacher understands you & have tutoring after school to help your grades, so if you're at this school, there is no reason to be failing this class.

From the time I've been in this class, you've always been professional and prepared. The daily work has always been written clearly on the board & the speeches you gave every day were relevant. You never missed a single day of school and you taught things that was related to what was going on in the world today and prepared us well for the FSA with the essays in class. Although the workload was big, you always explained it before we started & made things more easy. Your performance was good because you would start off serious & slip a little joke in to keep everyone's attention. This class helped me enhance my skills and I am glad that I had it.

—JP

==

May 31, 2017

Mr. Fishkind's performance on teaching is an outstanding 10. I thought English II was gonna be hard, but he explained it & taught in a way that I could understand it clearly. He has a way of using his own personal experience with life to help in what he's teaching or doing. He's always prepared for class and always outs in his grades on time. His performance this year has just been such a great thing to experience as a student. He's taught things that I never knew about or would want to learn but he made it interesting and fun.

The school year for me has been very interesting. I've gotten to experience cool, weird things in Biology I. I've learned a lot about the past in World History.

I've also grown more maturely as a person. This year wasn't so bad surprisingly, but I look forward to more great things to come the next school year.

—BT

///

May 31, 2017

This year went bye very fast. It felt like I had barly [barely?] enufe [enough] time to lear[n] but luckly I had good friends and teachers to help me out. This year all so has its moments like the funny joke that were made by me. In addition, I turned 17.

One teacher stood out from the rest that was Mr. Fishkind he was one of the best teachers 10/10 this year. Mr. Fishkind is very polite, light heat and respectful. I hope I can get another teacher like he next year.

—JT

And so concludes English 3. If you have a headache after reading these entries, I am not surprised. As I said, they were an unrefined lot, but there were diamonds in the rough.

And now on to...

Period 7
Intensive Reading

May 31, 2017

This year was honestly very challenging. I had to go through a lot of obstacles. I had many Honor classes that ended up being very hard. This year I had new friends that were always there for me.

I had also gotten very good grades however they could be better. My performance [yet another one who misread the prompt] is good. I actually believe I had enough points to pass the FSA. My teacher helped me to perform to my capacity and to end up passing. I believe that I am very proud of myself and that I am going to end up passing through High school!

—BA

May 31, 2017

My school year at Somerset friend wise was good but academic wise not so good. I was happy with some teachers, but most teachers not really. All they do is complain. Like they be so annoying. I was getting in so much trouble over there. So, it was time to go to another school. So, we decided to go to Everglades, and I came the last week of the 3rd quarter. Finished the rest of the year off here. I like it so much better than over there.

[Did not get the prompt]

—Unsigned

//

May 31, 2017

This year has had some ups and downs. This year has been a bit difficult only in my Spanish & Math class. It's really hard keeping up my grade in those classes. I've failed like every test & quiz in my Math class & Spanish class but towards the middle of the year I started studying then my Spanish test go up.

Oh Mr. Fishkind you get a miraculous 10 because you never change, and you always help us or 'me' out when I need it.

Thank you for being you.

—AD

==

May 31, 2017

This school year has been no different than any other school year. Over the past 9 months, I went through failing my classes, being shy in front of people, and trying my best to bring my grade up at the end of each quarter. But this school year, I've learned that not making friends isn't a big deal because by the time you finish High School, everybody goes their separate ways and that's why it's good to keep a small circle (of friends). I also learned that I need to take every year of High School seriously because my grade/GPA is very important and delicate and can determine whether I graduate or not. As a student of Mr. Fishkind, I rate his performance as a 9/10. Mr. Fishkind treated all his students the right way just like he was supposed to. He would explain the work more than he was supposed to, he would make sure everyone understood the lesson, and he did everything he possibly could to help us pass the Florida State Assessment. Although he would give us 2 to 3 class periods to complete assignments, Mr. Fishkind would load us with a ton of work. For the amount of work he assigned, the word 'Intensive' is an understatement. But at the end of the day, I understand the reason for all this is for our work ethic to grow and for all of us to be smarter and pass Reading.

—GD

//

May 31, 2017

This school year has been fun for me. I met a lot of new friends this year. This school year went by pretty fast. I like all my classes all my teachers they were fun and exciting. I like the experience of this school year,

I also like the football experience. It was good I learned a lot of new valuable things. It was a lot of hard work and dedication. I am very excited to be a part of Everglades next year. It's going to be a better year and be a part of new activities get improved in more things.

—LD

And another who missed what the prompt was all about.

==

May 31, 2017

This school year for me has been well but I kinda learned a lot. I've learned that even the closest people can be the main cause of all negativity in your life. Sometimes it's best to remove yourself to get back on the right track, and keep your head in the game, even when people try to knock you off. I've gotten closer to those I least expected and far from those I least expected. My grades were well but next year I know I'm going to do much better especially because I chose all Honors.

In my personal opinion, I think my teacher, Mr. Fishkind, professionalism, preparedness and performance was good but way better than most of my other teachers.

Even when certain students were annoying, he'll have an intelligent comment prepared to say without getting out of character.

—JF

///

May 31, 2017

This school year has been a fun and stressful experience. As most people know I started a new school at Everglades High. I only been here for 4 months and it's been fun since I was home schooled for a few months. I missed the communication and faces of other students. I was open arms and even made a lot of close friends. It was also stressful because I had to deal with drama and my grades. Some classes were hard and sometimes the teachers didn't take the time to help me. But overall, I had so much fun. My teacher, Mr. Fishkind is one of my favorite teachers. He takes the time to sit and talk to you and he treats people how they treat him. As a teacher, he doesn't give hard work and he gives you time to do stuff and he lets you know beforehand when something is due. He is very prepared and organized before you get into class you should already know what to do. I feel prepared for the FSA because I learned what I needed to know by class discussions and vocabulary quizzes. My advice to anyone who has him next year is to not take advantage of your opportunity to become the best.

—JG

===

May 31, 2017

The school year this year was boring. I met no new friends, and the lunch was nasty. The classes I had this year was good, all except one. My eighth period teacher was a real pain in the rear end.

I maintained a good grade for the first two quarters. My grades were horrible.

—XG

Perhaps if this student had not treated their "bathroom" trips like a concert where there were lots of stuff being smoked, they would have had more focus and done better—but not this one.

//

May 31, 2017

This school year has been good although my grades haven't. when I say it's been good, I mean it was fun. The class wasn't too hard I just don't focus or pay attention when I should. I've also learned a lot this school year. In my classes my teachers made me read to I improve my fluency while reading out loud.

Mr. Fishkind's performance for this year has been very good. He is very professional. A good example is his use of no cursing or want to go too far off topic. His performance is very good because he is always willing to help out his students and listens to us when we ask him to. My only complaint is when we are doing work, he stops us to do another task even though we were not finished.

—SH

===

May 31, 2017

My year has been pretty decent. Although I am not a big fan of school. I have improved a lot. Improvement in studying habits, socialization and confidence has gotten me through this year without any trouble. This school year of High School might have been my favorite year, considering my 9th grade year at Miramar High was pretty miserable. My personality hasn't changed, a shy girl with a little more wisdom and a lot more strengths. You have been a great teacher. A great teacher who has educated, inspired and pushed us to work hard while making learning interesting. There has always been no pressure of force in students to learn or get work done. Time has always been well-managed, and work was always prepared and organized.

—JH

//

May 31, 2017

This year has been slightly more difficult than last year. I took AP Psych so there was a lot more work than I expected. I had to study which is something I rarely do.

Algebra 2 was also extremely difficult because I'm not good at Math. But other than those classes my year was I simple. All my other classes were easy.

Fishkind's performance overall was amazing. He has a great attitude. He prepared us correctly for the FSA. He is very motivated to help everyone, and it motivates me. I do wish his class was more entertaining though. Overall, everything was helpful but just a little boring.

—LL

==

May 31, 2017

This year was very interesting. Moving to Florida gave me a different perspective on life. I learned that life is filled with disappointments. Also, life gets worse after High School. There is so much to dislike about this school. It's not the Math Department with incompetent teachers that gets me frustrated. Or even the school for taking a class I loved away from me. It's all the people in this school who believe I owe them something [!]

But now, it's about you. You have been really cool, honestly. You kept me in the zone throughout the year. You definitely are prepared. Our agenda is written on the board every day. Also, you were the most trusting teacher I met this year. You also somehow keep your composure throughout the year. That's my honest view of yourself.

—BM

///

May 31, 2017

My school year this year has been up and down. There has been days when everything is just downhill. I feel like this year I could have been way much better; with the things I do. But there have also been days when I'm happy and I'm on track. This year has contained a lot of emotions with me. Don't feel as if this year has been good for me. The good thing is this year is over, but I do want to put my education before everything and anything next year.

I feel like Mr. Fishkind has been there sometimes for me. Mr. Fishkind is a great teacher even though he talks bad about me [!]. my feelings were hurt when my friends told me what you said [!] about me. At the end of the day, you were a great teacher. The way you handled your class is awesome. I do feel as if you have done everything that is possible for me to be ready for the EOC.

—BS

When this student said I "talked bad about them," the incident was related to when this student was caught skipping class, and when asked where this student was, I mentioned that they were in school, but not in class. The truth can be painful.

==

May 31, 2017

This year has bene a roller coaster for me. Everything went up and down, but luckily everything finished perfect with good grades and scores. I've been stressed out every day but it payed off at the end. One of the main things I stressed over was all the EOC's and the FSA (Reading, Geometry, Biology). The hardest EOC I took was Geometry and I don't know what happened, but I completely forgot some things while taking it. I still have confidence that I will pass with a 3.

Moving on, Mr. Fishkind…your class has been the second most stressful thing in this school year! (just kidding) I really think all the work we've done has really gave me confidence to pass the FSA. I've learned a lot of reading skills and how to cite evidence for answering questions. I strongly believe I got a passing score!

Thank you so much for pushing not only me but the whole class. It has been a great second year at Everglades High School!

—IT

///

May 31, 2017

This school year has been a fun and awesome school year. From the fun activities I do every weekend to seeing 4 of my teachers 3 times in 5 days. I made a lot of friends this year and I had better grades then last year. I finally had got my license this year and my car. I had bought two dirtbikes and two jetskis. The experience I had with my new friends was awesome. We've gone so many places Key West, Ice Skating, jetskis, etc. I had learned a lot this year with all my teachers. All of my teachers this year were super helpful and cool. I hope that next year will be just as awesome as this year.

Mr. Fishkind rate: professionalism: 5 stars performance: 5 stars preparedness: 4 stars.

===

May 31, 2017

For me, this year has been very eventful and quite difficult. It's been very difficult for me because of some classes I took this year. For example, I made the decision to take AP World History, which was a bad idea cause it was something that was very difficult for me. Plus, this year was quite eventful for me because of the afterschool things that I participated in with drama. Also getting a ton of work each day it was just a lot to handle.

Mr. Fishkind performance overall is excellent. I actually think that at of all the seven classes that I have, I feel that I learned the most in this class thanks to him. But although he might gave us a lot of work. It is worth it because in the end it got us ready to take the FSA reading and writing. Overall, I'm really glad that had Mr. Fishkind as my teacher this year.

—BV

///

May 31, 2017

My school year this year has been a very crazy year. At first, I was doing very well staying on task doing my work turning it in on time I had great attendance and was staying on task, but my focus started to get mixed up. I was worried about the wrong things when I should have kepted my focus and stayed on top of my stuff and keep my grades in order and maintained.

Mr. Fishkind perforce is very well and maintained.

—CW

Remember I said these were unfiltered nor edited—raw as they were received?

==

May 31, 2017

This school year has bene up and down year my grades weren't the best, but they were okay. I felt like o could have done better with my grades and behavior. In some classes I did better than others. The really only class I struggled in was Math, and that's really it.

I feel like my 7ᵗʰ period teacher, the great Mr. Fishkind did a great job of teaching us and getting us ready for the exams and all of that. We had tonssssss of work, but it helped us at the end of the day.

—JW

//

Which brings us to eighth period. Ask any teacher which are their most challenging periods, and most will say the last ones of the day—and this group was no exception. Read and enjoy—raw!

Period 8
Intensive Reading

May 31, 2017

This year has been very stressful and hard. I struggled with keeping my grades up and had to work extra hard to stay on track. As you go up a grade it definitely gets harder. My gpa is still the same. I'm going to do summer classes to help it go up even more.

Mr. Fishkind's performance as a teacher was good. He encouraged his students to do better and be better students. He pushed us to the limit to achieve greatness he thought we could.

—TAC

//

May 31, 2017

This year has been very stressful with the amount of work given to the students. For example, my year had a Biology EOC. My year also went by really quickly.

World History was my only Honors class and I struggled with it. In my point of view, Mr. Fishkind's performance in professionalism and preparedness was excellent he was always professional and almost never yelled in class. Mr. Fishkind was always prepared for the students to get work and almost never gave homework. Mr. Fishkind's performance in class was also just as good.

—BA

===

May 31, 2017

What this year has been for me is great because I learned so much more things that I didn't know about. I also improved my grades this year by the help of my teachers. I mostly improved my writing and reading skills by the help of Mr. Fishkind and Mr. Vasquez. Now I know how to write and read almost professionally, and I am glad. I also learned new things in Math and the rest of my classes.

Mr. Fishkind's performance has been a magnificent job because he has made us do a ton of work which actually helped me in the end, and it was totally worth it. I have been able to improve my vocabulary thank to Mr. Fishkind, in terms of preparedness, Mr. Fishkind is in fire with this one because once we walk in the class, he already has the work on the board, and he tells us what to do in a very professional way. Mr. Fishkind's performance has been excellent because he is one of the few teachers that actually helped me improve in something by a lot. If I were to rate Mr. Fishkind, I would give him a 10/10.

—VA

//

May 31, 2017

Throughout this great long year, I have experienced and learned many things. This year has been great and very memorable. As every school year goes by more responsibility are added. But nevertheless, I have no regrets of what I have done. I've seen friends come and go but it proves to show you that your true friends will always stick by you no matter what the situation may be.

Throughout the year your performance has been phenomenal! Your professionalism was great although there were times you had your days. But it's okay because we all have our bad days. But besides the point you did an excellent job in getting us prepared. You demonstrated persistence and determination to get us where we need to be. I appreciate all that you have done for us. I will definitely visit you next year. Thank you, Mr. Fishkind.

—SA

==

May 31, 2017

This year has been filled with ups and downs. This year was the worst I've done in school [yikes!] I've realized a lot since this school year has started. Not only have I gained friends, but I lost some as well. This year was very overwhelming and stressful. I've been doing terrible in Math and currently still am. Although this year has been hell, I've also learned many new lessons. Mr. Fishkind is not my favorite teacher, but he does care about his students and does a lot to help them. He does prepare students for the real world, that I can say. And he cares very much about his job, that he doesn't play about.

He may be a pain most of the time, but he always makes sure that his students are okay and that they have a passing grade.

—AG

//

May 31, 2017

What this year has been like is good because my grades improved drastically, and my teachers were way nicer this year and Fishkind has been helping me on my reading skills and writing. Also, Vasquez has been helping a lot when it comes to quotation and detailed answers. And especially Mr. Serrano, he has been the best teacher I have ever had in my entire life he taught me real-life situations and also Chemistry.

When it comes to professionalism Mr. Fishkind is that because he is always telling us to be on time and to do the work because if not in the real world we would be fired. Also, in professionalism he is always giving us tips in the business world. Also, when it comes to preparedness Mr. Fishkind is also that because he is always organized. Also, Mr. Fishkind is always on top of his work. And all the work we did this year as a lot, but it prepared for the real world. And if I were to give Mr. Fishkind a rate it would be a 10/10 because he prepared me for the future.

—GG

===

May 31, 2017

For me, this year has been very stressful even though I still have some things to work on. I've accomplished many of my goals, like maintaining a 4.0 GPA.

I've also been a good girl this school year by not fighting or being a part of drama, because that use to be my main problem. Last, my attitude towards others changed a little and I feel more than accomplish because many people use to say I was 'stuck up' but now I was able to meet new friends and interact with them. So overall this year has been okay for me,

If I was to rate your performance in terms of professionalism, I would say that it was 10 because you always help in times of need and make sure our students were ready for the standardized test. In terms of preparedness, I would say a 10 because you really worked our butts off, you gave us just enough work to help us pass the standardized test. If someone fails that'll feel really sorry for them. In terms of performance a 10 also because you made sure that we were ready. So overall your performance for this year 2016-2017 was great.

—AJ

///

May 31, 2017

For me, this year was amazing. It went by really fast, and I wish it was longer. I love school even though most teenagers despise it. School for me was a place of learning new things and experience after school activities. I can't wait for next year!!!

Mr. Fishkind, you are a great teacher. On a scale of 1 to 10, your professionalism and teaching is a 10. All you should change is the amount of time you give to do work in class. You should give students more time. Thank you for an awesome school year!!!

—BA

PS: Sorry for the messy writing. It's BA's fault.

===

May 31, 2017

Since the beginning of the school year, I have worked hard in all my classes. Throughout the year I have improved in all my classed including English, Geometry, AP Spanish and Reading. I have met new people every day and have become friends with them. Spending my weekends doing my homework and studying for any tests I had on my classes. Volunteering in the school and outside of the school.

Helping people around me who were confused or lost. Also translating for those who could not speak English. Taking classes online to get more credits before my Junior year.

In Mr. Fishkind's class, I have learned many things that can help me in the future. For example, I have learned things that will help me during presentations in school or when I have a job later on in life. This class has motivated me to try my hardest in life no matter what it is. Thank you, Mr. Fishkind, for everything you have done this year throughout the course. For motivating us to work harder in every class and never giving up.

—NM

///

May 31, 2017

This year has been a fun learning environment for me, and I feel like I am leaving as wiser person. I took advantage of this year to finish my science requirements for college and my online classes. This year I met new people and was able to get good grades through hard work and tolerance.

I am very greatful [grateful] for this year and the year to come. Overall, I think I have become a better student.

Dear Mr. Fishkind—your performance in this class was over expected level. You're a very professional man who is always on time and knows what do to with any or every situation. You were always prepared and ready to work no matter what. When people didn't know what to do you were always there to help, so thank you.

—RM

===

May 31, 2017

This year has been a ride actually. It hasn't been the best, but it wasn't the worst. I've learned about fake people and seeing who is really there for you when need a shoulder to lean on. I made really good friends though and I'm grateful for them. Another thing I've learned from this school year is that the school's breakfast is fake. I'm telling you it's made of plastic pancake mix. Now around to the greatest teacher alive, you, Mr. Fishkind. Even though you'd act moody & everything you're still one of the best teachers I've ever had. You've taught me about life lessons that I know I'll use later on in life. You're very professional though & you get a 5-star rating from me. All you need to work on is you're attitude when something happens & also how you manage your time. Other than that, you're an amazing teacher.

—AP

///

May 31, 2017

This school year for me was kind of hard. I struggled with a topic that I had never struggled in before. Overall, I passed all my other classes with A's & B's. I feel that all the late nights were worth it because now that summer is coming, I get to take a break.

Your performance as a teacher is really well. To me, you are very professional by the way you act & speak. You are always prepared for a class & you take your job extremely seriously which is well. I'll miss you as my teacher.

—AR

===

May 31, 2017

My school year has been ok. The reason I say it has bene ok is because I have been staying outta trouble but then school started getting boring cause people have been getting kicked out left and right and haven't been making al A's this school year [reality check—never did…have seen the transcripts…yikes!]

Mr. Fishkind performance as a teacher was annoying sometimes [had to wake this one nearly every day, especially after the bathroom break *cough*] but taught us a valuable lesson at times. But at the end of the day the class still learn the work he reviews & better our reading skillz.

—MS

//

May 31, 2017

Throughout my 10th grade year at Everglades High School, I've learned so much and accomplished a lot of things in all my classes. For example, how to be a better student and how to finish and turn in my work on time. And y doing those things I've passed all my classes and also got straight A's. I had to do lots more and pay attention in class to get those things but at the end of the day it was all worth it.

Dear Mr. Fishkind, thank you so much for everything you have taught me and also ways I can be a better student. This year in your class has been a blast for me. I've learned so much. And also accomplished so many goals that you helped me set this year to be a better student. So again, thank you so much, and if I have any problems in school. To talk about the issue. You friend,

—JS

===

May 31, 2017

At first my goals for this year was to get straight A's. That didn't go as planned. I kind of slacked off this year. I underestimated the amount of work I'd be doing this year. It was indeed stressful and tiring for me. But I enjoyed my Sophomore experience a lot. Can't wait till it's finally over.

Mr. Fishkind was a great teacher. He taught me a lot over the past school year. He taught me a lot about school and life. This class was not what I expected at all. But I'm glad I had a awesome teacher like Mr. Fishkind. Please excuse my handwriting.

—TS

//

May 31, 2017

This year has been filled with many ups and downs. One of my downs was when my grades kept dropping whenever I get to bring them up. Some ups about this school year was sports, specifically football. I did very good, and I went up to varsity spring and had good practice all the time. When the spring game came, I didn't have the game everyone expected me to. I could have done better but that game just wasn't my game. That was another down factor. Based on Mr. Fishkind performance I would rate his professionalism as a 10/10 he was just the right amount not too much & not too little. He wasn't too strict and made sure we did wot we needed to. Preparedness was 8/10 he always had us working and getting better in reading.

===

May 31, 2017

This year has been cool for me. My grades are on and I barely got in trouble. This year I learned a lot then I leaned last year. Everyone always say how good this year has been for me. Me and my teachers were cool, and they treated me well. This year I made money and lost money [!] free kem and free R they won't see them until next year. [not sure what is meant by this.] Mr. David Fishkind performance in terms of: professionalism, preparedness and performance is one of a kind. You wouldn't find a lot of teachers like him. When I first met him I though he was related to Albert Einstein. And I though the work he was giving us was bullshit but it helped me in the FSA. Mr. Fishkind is old but very active.

Also, he gives good advice.

David Fishkind is a cool dude.

—MT

As I have stated, this is unfiltered work as I want the authenticity to be unquestionable.

///

May 31, 2017

This year was definitely a roller coaster for me. So much happened in my life, with my family, with my friends & even with myself. My classes were really good. I did good in school to try to fix my gpa & the whole school year I didn't get more than 1 'C' & I am really proud of myself for that. But other than school my life is a mess. Friends come & go people become fake. It is a part of life, we move on.

Mr. Fishkind's performance was very good. I've never had a teacher like you. I love your personality & you're very well spirited. I love hearing your stories & your jokes. They aren't that funny but the way you say them is funny. You were always prepared & always had work to give us. Which obviously I'm not happy about but it's good how serious you take your job & yeah you were fun.

—MT (Different from other)

===

May 31, 2017

This 2016–2017 school year has been a rocky one. This school is always filled with drama and you somehow always get pulled in it. Like this girl Alex who said I called her a hoe when I didn't.

She talked so reckless and so much mess to my friend but when it came time to fight me, she was scared and didn't fight me like she said she would. One of the things that I wish I did was run track that I trained for over the summer but got distracted and didn't run for the school. Another thing that happened was I lost a good 'friend' of mine over a petty argument that had nothing to do with me except her and her girlfriend and two guys I know. I'm glad that I was shown what her true colors was. I made new friends and better friends.

Mr. Fishkind was my only teacher who really cared about my grades and wanted me to pass his class. He made sure that we always kept our grades, even though sometimes he yelled he still cared about his students, and their well-being. He always told us stories and life lessons as the days went on. I'm glad that I had him as a teacher.

—CT

//

May 31, 2017

This school year has been a good year, one to remember. Academically wise, it's been fairly easy but it's the end of the year now. Study Hall has been a useful to do makeup work in or homework. World History class has taught me a lot as well, My English teacher taught me how to cite evidence better. My coach for basketball has helped me get better at everything. Biology showed me more about the world. Geometry was a hard class that I sadly did not pass. [You and a lot of other folks…] Firefighting class has been one of the main factors in my life. Then to finish off I have your class.

Mr. Fishkind the performance you gave a s a teacher was a great performance. As a teacher, you gave us a lot of work. If you could have taught more, it would have been better. Honestly, the less work you would have gave us would have been easier [it is called Intensive Reading for a reason…] Next year, for the sake of your students to pass your class, lay back on the work because it's not really teaching us students anything.

—BV

===

And now on to the letters for this year—enjoy!

///

May 2017

Dear Mr. Fishkind,

I would like to thank you for all that you did to help me and my brother during my Sophomore year. You gave us some very good advice to the both of us. I hope that the next time I come to visit you, it would be as a proud United States Marine. It will be a difficult challenge but out of all my teachers, I am sure you're the one that will understand how difficult it will be to cut off my hair. I wish you the best and hope to see you again.

Thanks again,
KA
Class of 2017

May 2017

Dear Mr. Fishkind,

I would like to thank you for giving me the opportunity to have been a student of yours, my Sophomore year, in you Creative Writing class. You are a teacher I won't ever forget because you allowed students to express themselves, and without any judgement on your part, as well. You embody this quality in which your spirit isn't defined so much as you age but rather through substance. You viewed students as individuals, and didn't see them as ignorant because of their age, but rather you understood that they all had voices, and that they would like to be heard. I suppose you're a teacher I can't forget because I see a mirror of myself in you, and I wish to portray this everlasting care-free energy that you give off (but also because you're a Capricorn). Although we didn't talk too much, when we did, you were both easy and comfortable to have discussions with. Also, I was much shyer when I was a Sophomore so, any attempt someone made to talk to me was noticed by me. Id' like to think you had an influence on who I am today, since you would point out my qualities and wouldn't mean it in a and way, but rather different. I wish you well in your future endeavors, and I think you deserve nothing but the best.

Sincerely,

RQ

//

May 17, 2017

First, a big thank you!

Throughout my Sophomore year, I was guided with your creativity and support. You were my English teacher yet, the lessons I learned from you extended beyond the classroom. You always took the extra mile to help others, even ones who weren't ready to help themselves. I feel like you have always noticed one's potential and attempted to help them prosper. Although there were times when I slacked or procrastinated, you never gave up on me.

Thank you, Mr. Fishkind, for genuinely caring for others. I am so appreciative of the impact you have made during my high school career. I will continue to grow with your guidance in mind throughout the rest of my life. The learning environment you created was always fun and comforting! I especially enjoyed walking into class and hearing great music playing to start the class off right. The effort you put into motivating and teaching us was so apparent. I wish you nothing but the best in life because you deserve the same gratitude that you have shown me.

With much love and appreciation,

AJ

May 2017

Dear Mr. Fishkind,

You were the reason I was able to survive my beginning stages of high school. I never felt judged by you and I was able to tell you my deepest secrets and feelings. You were my psychologist that I needed, but for free. You always have kept your arms open towards me and I have always felt willing to come and speak to you, even on your worst of days. You have helped me grow as a person, and to not deteriorate myself so much as I have in tough situations. You have taught me to keep fighting, to never give up, and mostly:" this too shall pass."

I thank you so much for being there for me when I needed someone the most. You're one of a kind, Mr. Fishkind.

Much love,
NG

///

April 29, 2017

Dear Mr. Fishkind,

I remember the first day I was in your class, that day I said: "oh, this class is going to be pretty hard" but I also noticed you were a very good teacher and a good friend. Mr. Fishkind, I wrote this letter because I just wanted to say thank you for being a good teacher and for supporting me since the first day of my Sophomore year.

Thank you for this amazing year,

—RF

School year 2016–2017 was, as previously stated, a transitional year as the school changed from seven periods to A/B block scheduling, where we saw students every other day instead of every day, which somewhat altered the bonds that could be developed between students and teachers. The changes in my courses also contributed to the change in dynamics as well. But wait, just when you think all the changes are done, wait for 2017–2018. Ch-ch-ch-changes kept on coming as English classes were no longer part of my responsibility. Goodbye English and enter credit Recovery. Credit recovery, for those who are not familiar with the course, is an integrated English and history class where students, who, at some point during their early high school careers, managed to fail a course, have the opportunity to trade an elective course for credit recovery. Students then have the chance to "recover" their lost credit on the way to graduation. Credit recovery replaces "summer school" which was the way credits were recovered in the past. In order to instruct the course, the teacher must be certified in *both* subjects (English and history) for the grades to be accredited, and it necessitated I take the history (social science 6–12) exam and pass it to add to my teaching certificate. And so I did. With the addition of the social science subject area to my teaching license, I became one of only four teachers in our faculty to have two subject area license and two endorsements (reading and ESOL).

<hr/>

Period 3
Intensive Reading (2017–2018)

May 24, 2018

Mr. Fishkind is a kind, respectful knowledgeable instructor. His uncanny ability to keep cool and manage any situation is outstanding and shows his professionalism. Mr. Fishkind is a very knowledgeable teacher, always telling us about is life and even explaining experiences especially being physical, emotional and mental. These events show his personality. Mr. Fishkind also has a good sense of preparedness, he always did his best to make us prepared for the EOC, final and tests and quizzes. Every day was prepared with education. There was not a day Mr. Fishkind kept us waiting.

—B

///

May 24, 2018

Professionalism—I think you are really professional and when a problem presents to you about a student you resolve it and also give second chances and that's good. And you also help students in every way that you can and that is something that not much teachers do.

Preparedness—you are always prepared for every class and always leave us with stuff to do and I like that not always we have homework unless we didn't do it in class.

Personality—you are always making jokes and are happy most of the time and always interact with us. You are always engaged on everything we do.

—YC

May 24, 2018

Well basically I dislike this class because I really don't know anybody in this class but for you as a teacher. Basically, you're not like most teachers that yell and scream but as the times I've bene in your class. Everybody says your name and you can hear them but the time I call your name I have to call it more than once for you to hear me and I don't like that. But other than that, I don't have a problem with you.

—I

///

May 24, 2018

Personality—your personality was very calming. It takes a lot to push your buttons. So, it's good to be able to control your emotions even though some kids are hardheaded.

Professional—Your teaching was easy, but I wished you let us use our phones...

Preparedness—you always have the same routine. So, it was easy to know what to do.

—JL

May 24, 2018

Personality—so Mr. Fishkind this year I thought you were going to be so boring. But as class progressed, I learned that you are a really good teacher.

Professionalism—you are very professional. I see that you get all of our grades in right away.

Prepared—always letting us work and there is always an assignment ready for us to do so we can't fail but we can raise our grade.

—JL

//

May 24, 2018

Professionalism—Mr. Fishkind is a very fun teacher to have, but he always is about work first and talk and have fun after,

Preparedness—every day when I walk into Mr. Fishkind's class he always has the entire class planned out, and a description of the Achieve/wb progress we're about to do.

Personality—Mr. Fishkind's personality is one of the best I've ever seen in a teacher. He's really funny and has many life stories that are actually interesting.

—AM

May 24, 2018

Personality—Mr. Fishkind is a nice, funny guy I like his personality it's interesting.

Preparedness—he is always ready and prepared for whatever we doing like test, quiz…

Professional—he is really professional with his work and he is quick to grade and give you a reason why you failed or passed.

—I

///

May 24, 2018

Personality—9/10 you have interesting and funny stories about your life and what you've been through. It intrigues me some of them are sad, but you still create humor through it.

Professionalism—10/10 you are serious and mature when needed to be, you can act very profound and professional at any time.

Preparedness—9/10 you have work for us all the time and that's what I like and not too much work as well, just enough to make the day go by.

—P

May 29, 2018

I think you're a wonderful teacher and it shows that you care about the students too and not just about the pay. I like how I can trust you and I never have to worry or ask you to put my grade in pinnacle you always do it fast without me reminding you and you never killed my hopes and dreams like certain teachers have.

And I like how you never not once raised your voice on me you're like the grandpa I never had, and I hope to see you next year I feel like I could go to you when I'm sad and that's something I really appreciate about your teaching.

—JP

Quite a sentence here in this entry—it never fails to amaze me to see the effects I had on students.

///

May 24, 2018

5 facts why Fishkind is great

1. Fishkind is a person that make your day great and happy to come to his class when he greets you at the door.
2. Fishkind is a great guy that will help you with everything you have in problem with.
3. Fishkind is an understanding person if you need to go to another class to do something.
4. Fishkind is a person that will care for you just like if we were his kids and will help you to the end of the world.
5. Fishkind is an understand person that will help you and will give you extra time if you need it.

—R

Sometimes it is a challenge to live up to one's billing.

May 24, 2018

Personality—3 I feel like you're really funny and interesting. You're not like any other teacher here!

Preparedness—3—you've kept us prepared for everything through the school year.

Professionalism—3 you're professional in your own way.

—JR

//

May 24, 2018

1. I like your teaching style because you don't only talk about reading but other topics.
2. What I like about your personality is that you're outgoing and not afraid to speak your mind.
3. My opinion about your professionalism is that you're already a professional and when you teach, I actually think about my life more.

—LR

Period 4
Intensive Reading

May 24, 2018

I would rate Mr. Fishkind in personality a 10 out of 10. He is funny, he is always trying to help people for the better. He is actually really funny; he makes a lot of jokes that are actually funny. And he is very kind because I know that if I ever need him, he'll be there to help.

I would rate Mr. Fishkind a 10 out of 10 professionally because he is always ready to give us lessons and its always professional about everything.

I would rate Mr. Fishkind a 10 out of 10 in preparation because again he is always prepared for everything and is ready for a lesson and something to teach.

—NA

May 24, 2018

Mr. Fishkind you're a good man when you come to school your very appropriate you dress appropriately, and you show to everyone the way you like to be treated. If I rate you from 1–10, I would give you 7 but that is because I don't like coming to school but you should continue your journey as a teacher. #1

—C

//

May 24, 2018

Performance is a 9 out 10 when it comes to professionalism, I think your very professional. You don't argue with kids and a rea big people person. You always have everything on the board. You know what we have to do & gives us time to finish the work. Your personality is good you are very outspoken & is always happy. You never let things get to you & you always give many 2nd chances.

—KC

May 24, 2018

Preparedness—he always has work set out for us and is always making sure were busy.

Personality—he's really funny and nice never has to raise his voice.

Professionalism—he is very professional.

—SF

//

May 24, 2018

Mr. Fishkind: teacher rating from 1–5 stars—5 stars
An interesting and good teacher definitely not boring like other teachers. This class was pretty easy. Though a lot of the work was interactive with the students. A good teacher overall.

—AGS

May 24, 2018

I rate you a 10 on a scale of 1–10. Sometimes your jokes are really cringey and NOT funny…but you're pretty cool and a showoff type smart. You're kind and professional.

Sincerely,
AG

//

May 24, 2018

I think your personality is great. You help your students with the best you can. I like your jokes; I feel comfortable whenever I come to your class. You are professional, I like the way you teach, your works help m. you make school a little reading skill a lot. I feel my reading skills are improved.

—AL

May 24, 2018

To the coolest teacher ever!
Personality—as far as personality goes I for one think your personality is great. You are very understanding and nice. Sometimes I

have my bad days but when I come to your class you never fail to make me smile or laugh. You've made reading easy and fun. I've really enjoyed your class this year. You are one of my favorite teachers. You make school a little less suckish.

Professionalism—you are very professional although you are our teacher you take time out to know us on a personal level beyond students. You actually care about what goes on in our lives outside of school. Unlike most of the teachers at this school you didn't make our lives a living hell. For that I truly thank you.

Preparedness—I can't remember a time when you weren't prepared for class. Every time I came to class you were ready to tell us the theme of our Achieve story then our workbook pages and so forth. You aren't one of those teachers who is all over the place.

—JL

//

I am not sure if anyone has ever said this, but a child cannot learn unless they have a peaceful place in which to do so. I always believed in the power of connection. If a student feels a sense of connection with a teacher, they will make more of an effort on a given task, even if they do not like it much. I have always treasured the fact that I know my students, and they get to know me.

May 24, 2018

Mr. Fishkind is very responsible at his job. He never miss a day of school. He makes a lot of jokes; he makes the class fun. He's cool and I can sincerely say he's one of the best teachers I ever had.

—JR

May 24, 2018

Preparedness—10—ever since got here he has always been prepared.

Personality—10—he is very nice and funny also very helpful.

Professionalism—10—he is always professional; he is corny every now and then, but he stays on task to help us learn.

—RS

May 24, 2018

Mr. Fishkind can get very funny & playful but when it time to work he can get as professional as a lawyer, always make sure were learning about something new every day. He has a lot of experience, so he was able to teach a lot. Never missed a day but if he has to, makes sure we have lots of work to do & learn about the story.

Personality wise loves to make his kids laugh or leave them in question & tends to have a same companion as his kids such as basketball, traveling, etc.

—GW

Period 5
Intensive Reading

May 29, 2018

I rate you a 7.8 because you had personality and tried to make this stuff interesting even though it wasn't as fun as you tried to make it.

You prepared me quite a bit always reminding me of my work I need to do and giving me time to do it to improve my grade and you were very professional and did the job the government wants you to do to prepare us to be brainwashed by the government.

—CC

Yikes! I think this student has read one too many dystopian society novels.

///

May 29, 2018

I have learned to comprehend more since being in your class. It has taught me to have responsibility and to do better in my English class.

—AC

At least I was not preparing this one to be brainwashed…sheesh.

May 29, 2018

Professionalism—a very good teacher, one of the best I've had so far—very good at teaching the subject.

Preparedness—prepared us very well—taught us most of the stuff that was on the FSA—really good with vocabulary words

Personality—very understanding—a lot of patient [patience?] a lot of consideration

—KC

//

May 29, 2018

Mr. Fishkind performance was extremely good. He is very patient with students. He also retrains the fundamentals of reading, allowing students to remember the simple times of reading, but if I had to rate him on a scale, I would put him at 8–10.

—SD

May 29, 2018

Professionalism—9—gave us a lot of work to help us on the F.S.A.

Preparedness—10 always here on time and always have thing ready for anything.

Personality—8—you very funny a sometimes.

—SD

//

May 29, 2018

The whole year you were a great teacher. You showed me professionalism on how to be a brave and confident person. And you also gave me preparedness for life and school. You told me a lot about how to be successful in life and very wise. And last but not least, your personality. It showed how a person supposed to be. And I learned a lot from you Mr. Fishkind and I will be visiting you a lot when I'm out of school.

—DH

May 29, 2018

Professionalism: 9—you're a really good teacher, and you make to work easy for us to understand.

Preparedness: 10—because you are always prepared with paper or a pencil to give me when I need one. Your work is always on the board for us to look at and do.

Personality: 8—because you are always happy and in a good mood, but sometimes it's annoying when we are in a bad mood and you are trying to make us happier (not that it's a bad thing).

—ACM

///

May 29, 2018

Professionalism: You always let us turn in work late without complaints & always helped us.

Preparism: you always corrected us when we were wrong. You're always on time. Also, very detailed which was helpful.

Personality: I love your ties. You're a great teacher. I love your jokes.

—SM

May 29, 2018

Professional: 9—you were always very detailed and explained the work on Achieve. You gave us a brief summary before reading and it helped understand more. Even with late work you never gave attitude.

Personality: 10—you are very kind to us. I enjoy coming to your class. Your unique personality makes me enjoy the first period of the day. Love how you're always cracking jokes.

Prepare: 9—you always help us on days we're absent and try to bring our grade up. Though it's so much work, it's for a good reason, you're trying to get us out Intensive!

You will be missed!

—AP

//

May 29, 2018

You're a professional person—rate 10
You come quite prepared—rate: 8
Your performance is quite boring. You should be more lively in your classroom. Rate: 5 [!]

—TP

Really? A five? Boring? Come on.

May 29, 2018

Professionalism—10/10 for being very qualified.
Performance—10/10 for being ready to teach
Personality—11/10 for being friendly and signing my yearbook
Preparedness—10/10 for having our lessons planned out days in advance

—RP

May 29, 2018
Professionalism—8, Preparedness—7, Personality—8

Mr. Fishkind personality is 8 because his performance of personality help interact with others and with difficult situations.

Preparedness helps other be prepare in class, to help the student environment.

Professionals has help me to understand full academic requirements in Intensive Reading class.

—NT

//

And now on to sixth period—a bit of a wild bunch if there ever was one. There was one incident that particularly stood out. Students are not allowed to have their phones out in class, and I had one student who was a chronic violator of this policy. They nearly daily had their phone confiscated with requisite cursing, and it finally reached a point where the student managed to seize my laptop and hold it over their head while threatening to hurl it to the ground if I did not immediately give back their phone. Security was called, and the student was banished from my class permanently. They ended up leaving the school on an unrelated legal matter.

May 29, 2018

If anything went wrong, you never flipping out. You always acted according and handled it. 10/10

As for being ready for things is 10/10 because you always had us doing something. I can't recall one time I was sitting in this class and waiting to do something. 10/10

For me personal you seem like a cool guy. It's easy to talk to you and have conversations. 10/10

I have really enjoyed this class. Thank you for teaching me this year.

—MA

In my opinion, you have been an outstanding teacher. You have taught me things that I was a little bit aware about. You have also taught me to be more persistent with my work and my speech input. All in all, you been a really good teacher.

Sincerely,
CB

May 29, 2018

Performance professionalism: 10—you had high vocabulary & kept a hardworking environment

Preparedness: 10—you always had our assignments & test ready & in order.

Personality: 10—you are calm at certain times until the class pisses you off…

—ZB

May 29, 2018

Professionalism—he tried to keep a good working & quite [quiet] environment. Also, when he speaks to the class it's with very high vocabulary and seriousness. 9

Personality—he is very serious but nice and funny at times. 7

Preparedness—he was always prepared for each class and lesson. 10

—VD

May 29, 2018

Not to punish all when one does wrong…

I like your teaching you were very understanding knowing I didn't take the class before I came to the school which I appreciate. I had no clue they were going to stick me in the class. Professionalism was good he kept the teaching place great and quiet.

—DE

//

May 29, 2018

Based on professionalism I rate you (100%) because you keep things in order. I have never seen you slack off in class no matter what. You stay working and moving around.

In terms of being prepared you were always prepared for being prepared. I rate you (99.9%) because you always have everything ready and planned out for each class you have.

Personality I rate your personality (80%) because you have a good sense of humor, but you can be strict at certain times.

—TG

May 29, 2018

Professionalism: you are really professional because you handle most of the situations really well.

Preparedness: even if we are about to finish school we work because you want is to be prepared for our future and learn new things every day.

Personality: good teacher

—NH

//

May 29, 2018

Professionalism: during my 10th grade year, Mr. Fishkind has been the most professional teacher of my black days. [Our schedule for the A/B block scheduling was divided by the school colors of silver and black] there's always been a line between class behavior and clown-like behavior in the classroom and just like every other class, there were rules that needed to be followed. Preparedness: only once did I face the problem of an assignment or anything else being not prepared in this class which shows that being prepared isn't much of a problem for Mr. Fishkind. Personality: as far as personality, Fishkind has an amazing one unlike many other teachers. Fishkind has a great amount of patience with his students. He greets us, asks about our well-being and even engages in conversation from time to time. All while making sure we still get out work done, of course.

Overall, one of the best teachers for this year.

—BL

May 29, 2018

This year Mr. Fishkind was one of the most prepared teachers I had. He was very professional no matter what happened he never lost his cool. And for performance he always on his work and he was never slacking.

—NR

//

May 29, 2018

Mr. Fishkind has been an excellent teacher with a complex set of vocabulary which his goal is to stimulate the brain of his students. He also provides students with material and goes over material to prepare us, his students, for his tests. He has also been fair and tries helping his students the best he can. He also teaches at a rate where his students have a fair amount of time to complete their work and also accepts it even if it's late. If I had the chance to have this teacher again, I would gladly take it.

—JT

May 29, 2018

From a scale of 1–10, you are a 10. You're always prepared for class and always keep us on tasks. When a student is struggling, you're always the first one to help. You're the nicest teacher ever because you would greet me every time you see me and help me on my work.

—XX

Period 8
Intensive Reading

May 29, 2018

Professionalism—you have been a really good teacher. I've never met a teacher that has ever been so caring and motivative and honest with his students

Preparedness—we walk into class everyday with something new to do. You have made my learning experience wonderful every day I learn something new…whether it's a word or it's about the real world.

Personality—we've all seen a side of you that has shown positivity. Although some days the class may be rowdy [there were thirty students in this class] or there would just be a day that isn't as great as the others, you always find a way to make every student feel at home & welcome. You have been the most respectful & honest teacher I have ever had.

—MA

//

May 29, 2018

Gracias por todo (thanks for everything)

Thanks for being patient, for showing your knowledge, for advice us, for make me sit next to a very annoying person (complaint) for being fair with us, for help us out with everything. You have been a nice teacher.

To be honest, after being in your class I feel a big improvement in my English and myself. I want to say thank you for that too.

Performance: excellent—I can't complain

Professionalism: you know what we need—you got the skills to reach

Personality: funny, nice, kind, etc. etc.

—AA

May 29, 2018

Professionalism: every day we come to class there is always something we have to complete, never busy work like most teachers, but a daily routine students are never confused and know exactly what their job is, and how its' completed. You make your rules very clear on what you want done every day.

Preparedness: every day we need a sheet of notebook paper to complete work, you provide the unprepared students with paper. There was never a day you did not have any paper. You make sure no student in your class has an excuse not to be successful.

Personality: your personality is honestly the best thing about you. It makes your class much better, I even looked forward to coming to your class every day to learn and read about something new. This might be an opinion to others, but you are the best teacher ever…and that's a fact.

—AD

May 29, 2018

Professionalism: your performance was great the whole year especially when you would make jokes. You are very professional because you were not one of the teachers that taught from the book you were making it fun, and I like that.

Preparedness: you always prepared with the tools we need to do our work and you were always.

Personality: you were very funny and would always talk to me about basketball which made it interesting in class. I had fun this year, have a nice summer.

—KD

May 29, 2018

Mr. Fishkind's performance was great and consistent. He always had something to teach.

Mr. Fishkind's professionalism was fantastic. He allowed nothing from outside his classroom affect his class.

Mr. Fishkind was definitely prepared for this year's go around; the rules prove it.

—AE

May 29, 2018

Mr. Fishkind's professionalism is entertaining because every day he finds things for us to do to get excited for learning and in case he aren't in school he leaves work for us to do if we weren't there to complete it.

—SI

May 29, 2018

Performance: Your performance as a teacher is phenomenal your laid back but you always follow the rules, and you know how to keep a class in order yet fun all the time.

Professionalism: you're a very professional teacher and you always go about situations the correct way.

Preparedness: you're always prepared when we walk into class there is always work ready for us to do, work that is essential.

—TJ

///

May 29, 2018

Professionalism: you are very professional, and you handle your class and business well.

Preparedness: you are always prepared to teach, you come in on time and never miss a day of school.

Personality: you have a great personality. You're caring and is always there for everybody. You are also very intelligent, and you know how to give advice to others.

—AJ

May 29, 2018

Professionalism—Mr. Fishkind you're by far the most interesting teacher I've ever met. When I say interesting

I mean it in a good way. You have a lot of good logic that you give us & I thank you for that.

Preparedness—I would say you make sure everything is prepared for us when we get to class, and I thank you for that. I would rate you for having everything prepared for us a 10.

Personality—I love your personality you're like a father to us especially the girls in the class. I appreciate that very much.

—JJ

///

May 29, 2018

Mr. Fishkind is very professional and always has his class in order. He prepared us for our state test but the lesson were repetitive and I lost interest quick. Also, he has a great personality and is very funny.

—AL

May 29, 2018

Professionalism—professionalism was good on certain days. For example, if you are bothered then you'll let it affect you teaching us. Sometimes we'll be joking around, and you'll sometimes take it overboard knowing we're joking, you'll still call home. Also, your suits. [?]

Preparedness—the way you prepared us for the FSA, I didn't like the stories, but it helped me pass the FSA. Also, you helped me prepare for other classes such as Spanish. You inspire me to get my work done in Study Hall.

Personality—you could relate to some problems. You try to give us the best advice. You are a cool teacher but work first. I can relate to you jokes or personal life. I'm still trying to find a way to watch "In Living Color."

—MM

//

May 29, 2018

Your performance as a teacher was phenomenal. You taught us many things. Your very under rated teacher.

At a professional level your great. Your always on point everyday you're here.

Your personality is good too. I don't exactly know how long you've been a teacher, but I do know how to keep high spirits every day is hard. Your wise and kind. You've always give me chances especially when I didn't want it. I thank you for that.

—EN

===

May 29, 2018

This class has actually been the only class I actually look forward to. This class is fin and the teacher, Mr. Fishkind, is extremely helpful. When it comes to professionalism Mr. Fishkind never breaks rules. He hasn't broken a single rule this year. When it comes to preparedness, he does everything on a schedule and has materials provided. Fishkind's personality is amazing. He is funny, smart and a realist. He is the most helpful teacher I've had and the best to talk to.

—AP

//

May 29, 2018

Based on the following school year as a student in your Reading class, I would say that my vocabulary and knowledge has increased tremendously. Your professionalism is a letter grade of an A because you manage the time to have the tolerance to put up with this foolishness of the students in class. Your preparedness is also an A because you try the hardest you can show up to school every day and there is always a new topic for the work that needs to be done. When I walk in the classroom, I already know what the work is and there is an assignment that will be graded every single class rather than not doing any work at all. Your personality is an A because you know all of your students and you try to relate o how the students behave. Although it is a classroom you know how to make the classroom fun for all of the students while also teaching the correct way.

—TS

===

May 29, 2018

Your professionalism in the classroom is excellent because you never make us slack, and you want us to succeed by giving different work every day.

Your preparedness was also good because you made sure that we always have supplies to use in class and get our work done.

Your personality was awesome. You keep us entertained and made us want to work when we get to class. Also, you made us laugh and have fun.

—KT

//

And so ends the end of year reviews for 2017–2018. If ever there was a watershed year, this was it. The world of education was forever altered on February 14, 2018 when gunfire shattered what should have been a peaceful Valentine's Day. The Stoneman Douglas High tragedy has forever altered how education is looked at by students, teachers, administrators, and parents. You will see this as the story winds its way down. And now the letters for 2017–2018. Enjoy!

You may have noticed that I also included the letters from 2018–2019 as well. There were no end-of-year evaluations of any note. There was much stress this school year after Stoneman. Code red drills put a damper on the entire campus. It was just not the same place. And 2019–2020 was, in many ways, *much* worse as the pandemic shuttered the campus from March 13, 2020, until late October. While everyone tried to maintain education, the pandemic has forever made its mark on our society. As the union steward for our campus, I faced many challenges in keeping the members informed as to what the district was allowed to do by the state. Those of us who felt that the measures being taken by the district were inadequate safety-wise due to interference by the state caused many to be rejected for their applications for remote teaching accommodation (over one thousand in one weekend, which included myself). This led to my early retirement in November of 2020 and to this book.

///

May 15, 2018

Dear Mr. Fishkind,

Although you were only my teacher for 1 year, you had a tremendous impact on my Freshman year! Your class inspired me to think outside the box, to see no limit when it comes to writing and those lessons have helped me throughout the next of my classes. Thank you for dealing with my horrendous handwriting, my constant talking through class, and all the drama! Your class was one of my favorite classes I've ever took. I feel like Creative Writing helped me learn not only the basic fundamentals of writing, but of life as well! This class helped me realize that no matter how outlandish my ideas are, they are not stupid!

Thank you so much Mr. Fishkind for influencing my life for the better!

—DM

==

May 15, 2018

To Mr. Fishkind,

Even though I was only your student for a short time during my first year of High School, I would like to thank you for giving me the confidence I needed to find in my writing and in myself. Especially now as I am torn between what I will choose for my college major, my career path and essentially my life. Your teaching has been a big part of why I have not stopped writing or loving poetry and literature. The writing I could have never shown anybody before I proudly put on display, even better, I now carry myself with the fiercest of confidence I can muster. While three years ago it was a struggle to even look people in the eye not only that, but from observing you as a teacher and as a person I have been able to learn the strength and power in being gentle and kind to others no matter what. I know many students feel comforted and understood jus by speaking to you. Whether it's for advice or just someone to talk to, you really bring true meaning into your students' lives. It's because of your teaching I have found it best not to shut myself off so easily from others. As I move on from High school, I will always do my best to remember the lessons you have taught me.

Sincerely,
AR

///

May 15, 2018

Dear Mr. Fishkind,

The day Mr. Horowitz assigned this letter, you were the first person I thought of. It's been a while since we've talked or even seen each other. I just wanted to let you know that the year I had you was some of the most fun I've had in an English class. I felt really lucky to have had you as a teacher. You always brought energy to the class and that was really convenient considering the fact that we had you first period. Thank you for always believing in me and my what I thought was subpar writing. Thank you for setting the bar so high for teachers. Thank you for teaching with your heart and all you have. I appreciate you and everything you've done for me even though you might not realize it.

—AB

===

May 15, 2018

"Till next time this isn't goodbye."

What doesn't kill me makes me stronger. Your work never killed me, but it did give me the idea that life won't be easy. I have to work hard for it. Your one of the few teachers that show they want the best for their students. I'm real thankful for you guiding me Mr. Fishkind. I'm going to miss you very much. Thank you for opening my eyes and giving me a bit of taste of the real word. The day I finish and make something of my life, I'll think of you cause you guidance is what led me there. I've never wanted you to be disappointed in me because it hurts me. So, one day in time when school is done, and I have made a career I hope to see you one day to tell you all about it and make you proud.

—MD

//

May 16, 2019

Dear Mr. Fishkind,

I'll keep this letter short since I want to get straight to the point. Thank you for assisting me through the years. Sophomore, junior and Senior year. I know I was a mess but thank you for dealing with it and trying to help me with my problems and give me advice to handle it. I know not everything happened my way but thank you for housing me in your classroom and helping me overcome those problems. I hope that you are still in the school in the future after I completed the goals in my life. I would want to visit you and tell you of all the successes in my life, and I'll do it over a cup of coffee. Especially the one you make since oy always made coffee prior to my period and it would always smell like coffee in your room.

Sincerely,
—JC

==

May 16, 2019

Dear Mr. Fishkind,

I know it's bad to judge people the first time you meet them, but the moment I walk in your classroom, you greet me with a smile that made me feel welcomed. And I knew that you would be the coolest teacher that I'll ever have. When you teach, I feel so indulged into the lesson. You teach with so much passion and I hope you know that you have inspired so many people and I know you will keep doing it. I've only been in your class for a year, but you have taught me great things about life and you also encouraged me to believe in myself. For that, I thank you Mr. Fishkind. Now that I'm leaving High School, I just want you to know that you won't be forgotten. Thank you for everything Mr. Fishkind. Take care.

Sincerely,
DD

///

May 17, 2019

Dear Mr. Fishkind,

When I enter your class on Aug 15th, 2018, I knew it was going to a really good yea. Though I don't speak in your class I really enjoy it. I'm writing this to say thank you for being an amazing teacher.

—AR

===

May 18, 2019

Dear Mr. Fishkind,

I just wanted to say, even though you're just my Study Hall teacher, I want to thank you for absolutely everything! You have honestly taught me soo much. Just with your life lessons and advice! Thank you for all your patience.

Much love,
AR (Different one from above)

───

I retitled the book *What I Learned from My Students* as they never ceased to amaze me with how my teaching and working with them had impacted my students. What I learned from them is just how far compassion, listening, caring about them, and seeing how the work we did could possibly impact the future. Teachers generally do not enter the profession unless they have "the calling." The old saying, "Those who can, do—those who cannot, teach," rings hollow as is borne out by the pages you just read. Students *are* the future, and it has always been (at least for me.) *Handle with Care!* and that kindness and understanding are two of the most powerful tools a teacher can employ.

All good things must come to an end. (Why?)

Thank you, and I hope you enjoyed all that was shared with you here!

The End

About the Author

David J. Fishkind was a teacher in Broward County, Florida, until COVID hit and forced an early retirement. He came from New England, specifically Greater Boston and has lived in Florida over twenty years. He started teaching in 2003 in Homestead, Miami-Dade County, teaching for seven years, and moved to Broward in 2011. Over the nine years he spent in his Broward County school, he taught primarily English/language/arts, as well as creative writing, intensive reading, and credit recovery. Whichever capacity he was required to work in, he always was a positive force and engaged students as completely as possible. In his spare time, he is an athlete (softball and golf), as well as an artist (guitar and writing), as well as having a very active interest in history. He lives in Fort Lauderdale with his wife, her son, along with their four dogs and a cat. Upon retirement, he wondered how he would get along without his students as he had learned so much from them, and he started looking over the letters and evaluations he had received over the years. When people asked why he left the corporate world for teaching, making half the income, this book tells that story perfectly.

CPSIA information can be obtained
at www.ICGtesting.com
Printed in the USA
LVHW030105090821
694770LV00004B/504